*What Am I Supposed to Do
with My Life?*

What Am I Supposed to Do with My Life?

ASKING THE RIGHT QUESTIONS

Douglas J. Brouwer

William B. Eerdmans Publishing Company

Grand Rapids, Michigan / Cambridge, U.K.

Wm. B. Eerdmans Publishing Co.

255 Jefferson Ave. S.E., Grand Rapids, Michigan 49503 /

P.O. Box 163, Cambridge CB3 9PU U.K.

www.eerdmans.com

Printed in the United States of America

11 10 09 08 07 06   7 6 5 4 3 2 1

Library of Congress Cataloging-in-Publication Data

Brouwer, Douglas J.

    What am I supposed to do with my life?: asking the right questions /

    Douglas J. Brouwer.

        p.   cm.

    Includes bibliographical references.

    ISBN-10: 0-8028-2961-9 / ISBN-13: 978-0-8028-2961-0 (pbk.: alk. paper)

    1. Vocation — Christianity.   I. Title.

BV4740.B76   2006

248.4   dc22

                                    2006004258

Contents

Acknowledgments

Writing — at least the writing that I do — has not been the lonely, solitary activity I had once imagined it would be. And this book, even more so than my previous efforts, has definitely been the product of collaboration. A number of people, in both large and small ways, have contributed to the writing and publication of this book.

Almost ten years ago, in the unlikeliest of circumstances (waiting in a terribly long line for a restroom at a wedding reception), a conversation about vocation began, and the idea for a writers' group was born. I am indebted to group members Michele Hemple and Patricia Locke, who have collaborated with me now on three books. Their encouragement and hard questions, always in the right amounts and at the right times, have made me a better writer than I was before that wedding.

The writing of this particular book spanned two churches. The church I served in Wheaton, Illinois, for thirteen years heard much of the content of this book, either in sermons or in adult education classes. I am more grateful than words can express for the encouragement and love I received from the people of this church. Their questions pushed me to think deeply about vocation and also, thankfully, helped me to see that I wasn't the only one who wondered about this subject. The privilege of serving that church has been one of God's good gifts to me.

The church I now serve, in Ann Arbor, Michigan, has also heard much of the content of this book. In an adult education class I taught soon after my arrival, class members listened, responded, and challenged as only Ann Arbor people can. Academic communities are known for their intellectual rigor, and this one is no exception. I am grateful to be a part of this learning environment, and already I sense that I am growing and developing in new ways because of the people of this church. The move has been a good one.

At an early stage in the writing of this book, my good friend Jim Luzadder read the entire manuscript with care and thoughtfulness. His comments and reflections have pushed me to reconsider several issues that I thought I had already resolved. His background as a therapist served to sharpen several of my observations about human behavior and motivation. I am especially grateful to him for pointing me in the direction of Viktor Frankl, whose insights about meaning in life have made a deep impression on me.

Lee Hardy, a philosophy professor at Calvin College, received an e-mail from me one day last year, and I suspect that for him it was out of the blue. He had written a book about vocation several years before, one that I had found helpful, and I asked if he would be willing to meet with me and answer a few questions. He was, and I am grateful to him for his willingness to spend time with a stranger seeking wisdom.

Pek S. Jo, a new friend from Ann Arbor, also graciously agreed to read the manuscript. His comments also helped to shape my thinking at several key points. Pek's training in both theology and psychology — plus our Princeton connection — has made our conversations about this book (always over Chinese food) deeply satisfying.

Finally, my thanks to Eerdmans Publishing and to the friends there who have shown me encouragement over the years. Mary

Hietbrink, my editor, has made the editorial process engaging and fun. Her questions about the manuscript have, in every case, enabled me to say more clearly and with greater precision what I intended to say. I am grateful for our collaboration.

I dedicate this book to my daughters, who are at that time in life when the sheer number of possibilities open to them makes vocational thinking seem daunting rather than exciting. My prayer for them is that they will continue to ask good vocational questions. And my prayer for myself is that I'll resist the urge to get in their way.

Introduction

I've been a pastor now for more than twenty-five years. I preach and lead worship, I teach, I go to meetings (lots of them), and I get calls from people who want to meet with me. Either I suggest that we meet at my office, or I suggest we meet for a meal — usually lunch, sometimes breakfast. Sharing a meal, breaking bread together, usually feels less formal, more intimate than meeting in my office.

In the course of my work over the years, I've listened to a lot of people talk about a lot of subjects. It's turned out to be one of the most enjoyable parts of my work. I've met many wonderful people, and I've learned a great deal from them.

As I reflect on all of this listening, however, it seems clear to me that the number-one subject people want to talk about is vocation. No other subject even comes close.

People seldom use that word, of course — or even its more familiar form, "calling." And yet, people seem to know the *meaning* of those words. They seem to know, perhaps intuitively, that their lives ought to mean something, that their lives *should* have both purpose and meaning.

So, they'll ask this question (or one much like it): What am I supposed to do with my life?

Early on, I became aware that the people I meet don't really expect an answer from me. They listen, of course, if I happen to offer one, but they really don't expect me to find their meaning for them. Asking the question, I've discovered, is a way for them to voice their own existential struggle, and most of the time I'm simply invited to listen in or to help them sharpen the question. Discussing the question with me is a way for them to understand it better, to get another perspective, or to find someone who understands.

And usually I find that I do. The questions sound similar to the ones I've asked myself.

In my experience, people ask this question at nearly every age and stage of life. Young adults certainly do, but so do older adults — and nearly everyone in between. I suppose that what I expected in my work was to hear mostly from people in their twenties, as they went through the inevitable process of sorting out their various life choices.

What I never expected to hear was a newly retired person say, "I wonder what God has in mind for me to do?" When that happened the first time, I knew that I needed to pay attention. Until then, I had always assumed that in retirement we no longer need to ask vocational questions. But I found out I was wrong.

We ask vocational questions for as long as we are alive. And asking vocational questions is a way of truly being alive — to God, to the people around us, and to ourselves.

So this is a book for seekers of all ages. It's meant to be a guide of sorts, but it's more than that. It's meant to help us ask good questions, pointed questions, questions that get us closer to hearing God's voice in our lives.

Vocation, as we'll see, is more than work, what we happen to do, how we make a living. Vocation includes all of life — everything we are, everything we do, everything we aspire to be. Vocation is a way of life — or better yet, the journey of life. We live best, I think, when we live in response to a call, to God's call.

Vocational questions aren't easy questions — but then lives well lived are seldom easy. Vocational questions are complex and challenging, pushing us to look deeply into ourselves, and also compelling us to look beyond ourselves. They compel us — or they *should* compel us — to search out what is truly *worthy* of our lives.

So let me ask you: What are *you* supposed to be doing with your life? What would be worthy of the life that you've been given?

🖋 CHAPTER 1   *What Am I Supposed to Do with My Life?*

Not long ago, after I announced to my congregation in Wheaton that I would be leaving to accept a similar position in Ann Arbor, a parishioner called to — what else? — make an appointment. He said he'd been intending to talk to me about something that had been on his mind, and now that I was leaving, he figured he should finally get it off his chest. He said he had already waited too long.

I knew him well, respected him, and had always considered him to be a serious, hardworking, and thoughtful person. He was fifty-nine years old.

After he took a seat in my office, he started to speak with a look of what I took to be near-desperation on his face. His body language reinforced the intensity of his words: "I'm really struggling." I could see that he was. "I don't know what I'm going to do with my life," he said.

After he relaxed a bit, we had a wonderful conversation, and when it was over, we hugged before saying good-bye. At the time I wasn't sure why that conversation affected me so deeply. Looking back, though, I know I heard something of my own struggle in his words. Earlier in my life I had thought a great deal about vocational questions. That seemed utterly natural and normal to me then, and it still does. What I found surprising — and even alarming at times — was to find myself thinking about those questions at mid-life.

The truth is, I've wrestled with vocational questions throughout my life. But after my twenties and thirties, I figured I was pretty much alone in my wrestling. Or I chalked up my questions to being a pastor. Pastors, I assumed, were *expected* to think long and hard about their callings, but other people weren't — and most likely didn't.

Called to Be a Loser?

Several years ago I wrote an article for a popular journal for pastors. The title — "Called to Be a Loser?" — was intended to be provocative, but the content wasn't. It was mostly a review of what most pastors already know — or should know — about vocation, especially pastoral vocations.

Ministry isn't easy, I wrote, and most of us wouldn't do it unless we truly *felt called* to do it. As a small but very real (for me) example of my ongoing struggle with my call to ministry, I mentioned my lifelong love for cars and how conflicted I felt over the recent purchase of a small red sports car. I badly wanted the car, but I was unsure how appropriate it would be for me, as a pastor, to own a car like that. Driving a sports car didn't seem to fit with the life to which I had been called. I felt that my identity as a pastor was at stake in some ways.

> Then I heard the voice of the Lord saying, "Whom shall I send, and who will go for us?" And I said, "Here am I; send me!"
>
> Isaiah 6:8, NRSV

The journal that printed my article almost always includes the e-mail addresses of its writers, along with photos and bits of biographical information. To my surprise, for the next *two years* I received dozens of e-mails from colleagues, most of whom I didn't know. They wrote to me — sometimes at considerable length — about their own far more serious struggles and questions. Some of those e-mails were heartbreaking. I answered each one, thanked them for writing, and encouraged them to find someone with whom they could continue the conversation.

On one level the number of responses was gratifying. I certainly learned that I wasn't alone. But on another level the volume of responses was somewhat distressing. Pastors may have the language and the tools to think about their callings in a way that others perhaps do not, but more of us than I would ever have imagined struggle with questions of vocation.

A COUPLE of years ago, I decided to preach a fall sermon series on vocation for my congregation in Wheaton.

Over the summer I read widely about the subject, which is one of the ways I like to prepare for a sermons series. But this time I even talked to people who had done scholarly work on the subject. I made appointments with college professors and authors, sat with them in their offices, and asked thoughtful and probing questions. I poured myself into the topic with an unusual degree of passion. This was more than research for a sermon series; this was in many ways a personal quest. I needed answers for myself.

I had hoped for a positive response to the sermon series, of course. But the strength of the response — like the response to my article — surprised me and even distressed me a bit. I quickly realized that pastors weren't the only people who wrestled with vocational questions.

Far more church members than I had anticipated followed the series with a deep personal interest. Those who had to be out of town on Sunday called the church office on Monday to ask for a copy of the sermon they had missed.

As the series went along, my calendar filled up with appointments. That fall I rarely ate a breakfast or a lunch at home. My words had definitely touched a nerve.

3

It's Not about You

Last year I was asked to preach the baccalaureate sermon during commencement exercises at a small Presbyterian college in a neighboring state. When the college president asked me what I thought I might speak about, I said that I'd been giving some thought to vocation (quite an understatement) and wanted to reflect on the subject with the graduating seniors and their families. He seemed delighted and told me that the school had, in fact, recently received a sizable grant to pursue the subject in more depth. He even directed me to the college web site so that I could read more about the grant and what the college was doing with it.

A few days later, however, after I had mailed my sermon title to his secretary, he called back. "'Called to Be a Loser' is quite a sermon title," he said.

"Yes, it is," I agreed, not offering any further hints about what I planned to say.

"Well," he said, hesitating, as though unsure about how to continue the conversation, "we'll be looking forward to what you have to say." The tone of his good-bye suggested that I should behave myself — or this might be my last invitation.

As far as I could tell, the baccalaureate service was a beautiful one, and no one seemed particularly upset with what I said. I tried my best to be humorous. And brief. At times I even tried to speak over the heads of the graduates, so to speak, to the proud families and faculty also in attendance. But my message, I thought, was blunt and to the point: The "loser" in my sermon title was a reference to Jesus, who, according to the Bible, lost everything, but gained the whole world. "Give yourselves away through lives of service," I told the graduates, "and you will have all the meaning and purpose in life you can handle. That's your vocation." Then I added, "Now all you need is a job."

More than a few students approached me afterward and said, "Thanks for those words." One graduating senior, in cap and gown, made a point of seeking me out and saying, "Thank you for your words. For some reason, our teachers are afraid to tell us that lives of meaning and purpose come from lives of service, even though we kind of expected that at a Christian college."

AFTER THESE experiences, it was certainly obvious to me that vocational questions are on the minds of many people, maybe even most people. The questions may be asked in different ways — pastors, for example, may have unique concerns — but lots of us have vocational questions.

So why are the answers so hard to come by?

I think I know. Vocational thinking is countercultural. It flies in the face of the message we receive daily from popular culture, which insists again and again that happiness and contentment in life can be found in gratifying our own desires and seeing to our own needs. Even the way the vocational question is often framed reveals the importance our culture places on the self: "What am *I* supposed to do with *my* life?"

> God calls people to himself, but this call is no casual suggestion. He is so awe inspiring and his summons so commanding that only one response is appropriate — a response as total and universal as the authority of the Caller.
>
> Os Guinness, *The Call: Finding and Fulfilling the Central Purpose of Your Life*

Rick Warren, a popular pastor in southern California, wrote a best-selling book entitled *The Purpose-Driven Life,* which begins with this sentence: "It's not about you."

I agree, but what's astonishing to me is that a book with that sentence as a starting point and premise has sold millions of copies. We don't often hear someone take that position. Popular culture tells us that it *is* about us. But people of faith know — or should know — that it's not about us. We have been called to love God *and* to love our neighbor as ourselves. We have the ultimate example of Jesus, who gave his life for us.

Our chief end in life is not to gratify our every desire, but, as the Westminster Shorter Catechism reminds us, to "glorify God and enjoy him forever."

Something Bigger than Ourselves

In my reading about vocation, I've found a number of helpful and compelling books, many of which I've noted in the bibliography. In recent years, one author in particular has written in an especially engaging way about vocation, and he's found a wide audience for his insights and ideas. Although he speaks to many, his tone is warm and personal. His name is Parker Palmer.

In one of his more recent books, *Let Your Life Speak: Listening for the Voice of Vocation,* he encourages readers to pay attention to what their lives are saying as a way of discerning their calling in life. Listen to your life, he says.

On one level, of course, I see the wisdom in that advice. I think that paying attention to our gifts and life experiences is a critically important step in the discernment process. I doubt that I would be in parish ministry today if I hadn't done a careful assessment of my gifts and interests, if I hadn't listened, as Palmer says, to my life.

Beyond that, I'm aware that early Christian mystics urged people of faith to listen for the voice of God within, and so from the earliest days of the church, Christians have practiced the discipline of being attentive to God's voice and direction.

And yet, I have to say that something about the "listen to your life" advice troubles me. It's not that God doesn't speak to us in this way — but is the message compelling enough? I like burning bushes rather than still, small voices.

When I think about vocation, I think about something far bigger than myself. I think about something far bigger than what my inner voice might be telling me. I think about something far bigger than my own dreams and ambitions. I think about . . . well, I think about God. I think about God's plan. I think about how I might fit into that plan and be a part of it and participate meaningfully in it. I think about God calling me beyond myself to places I would never have considered on my own. That kind of call is so powerful and filled with purpose that it can only come from outside me.

To me, being called implies that there is something or someone beyond myself — in other words, that there is One who calls. When I am called, I am summoned or compelled to respond. I participate in the call, of course, through my response, but there's a sense in which I couldn't say no, even if I wanted to.

When God calls people in the Bible, they're often surprised. Being called was the last thing on their minds. Often they resist. Sometimes they're terrified. And they almost always complain that they're not up to the task. They see, almost immediately, that God's call will take them in an entirely different direction from the one they had in mind for themselves.

> Then Moses said, "I must turn aside and look at this great sight, and see why the bush is not burned up." When the LORD saw that he had turned aside to see, God called to him out of the bush, "Moses, Moses!" And he said, "Here I am."
>
> Exodus 3:3-4, NRSV

To our way of thinking, God calls the least likely people. Moses was a murderer on the run. David was a lowly shepherd and the youngest of his brothers. Mary was a young peasant girl from Nazareth. And yet, God saw something in each of them that no one else could see. And when they didn't have what was required, God equipped them and gave them exactly what they needed.

Convince Me

As a preacher, I am keenly aware that the church no longer enjoys a dominant position within popular culture. In my childhood it did, but no longer. In my lifetime, the church has been disestablished. For most people, the church — and the faith it proclaims — is irrelevant. When I preach, I can no longer assume that my hearers will be in general agreement with what I have to say. Few of them regard the Bible as the truth — one source of truth among others, perhaps, but not *the* truth.

Most Sundays I speak to congregations that are full of seekers, people who are open to Christian faith but who don't fully embrace it. I sense that they want to be persuaded; they're open to what I say. But they're also skeptical. Their arms, in a figurative way, are folded across their chests, and the signal I receive from them is clear: "Convince me. Show me that I should care."

I write these words with those same seekers in mind, the same people who come to my church week after week, the same open but skeptical, hoping-to-be-persuaded people. I have come to see that my own calling in life, my vocation, is speaking to you, making sense for you of my own deeply held faith. In my preaching, teaching, and writing, I do my best to pass on the faith that I myself have received, but in fresh language.

After a lifetime of asking vocational questions, I'm convinced that my faith has compelling words to speak about the subject, words that deserve a hearing, words that have made a difference in my own struggle.

You should know, right up front, that what I believe about vocation swims against the current of popular culture. And for that reason, what I believe and what I have to say to you in this book may be difficult to hear: *It's not about you. It's about the One who calls you. Beyond that, God's call is often demanding. It will require sacrifice of some kind, and possibly some hardship. But it will result in meaning and purpose. You can be sure of that.*

But, difficult to hear or not, I believe these words deserve a hearing. The Christian faith provides a compelling answer to a question that many, many people are asking.

What are you supposed to do with your life? Do you know?

QUESTIONS FOR REFLECTION AND DISCUSSION

1. The Bible is filled with stories of call. In this chapter I've mentioned Moses, David, and Mary, but there are many others who hear God's call in their lives and respond to it. Read a couple of these stories and notice both what they have in common and how they are different from each other:

    Abraham: Genesis 12:1-9

    Joshua: Joshua 1:1-9

    Samuel: 1 Samuel 3:1-18

    Jeremiah: Jeremiah 1:1-10

    Ezekiel: Ezekiel 1–3

    Simon, Andrew, James, and John: Mark 1:16-20, Matthew 4:18-22

    Matthew: Matthew 9:9

    Paul: Acts 9:1-18

2. What are some of the vocational questions that you've asked in your life? Did you talk about them with anyone? Did you read something that you found helpful? What process did you go through as you wrestled with your questions? Did you come to any conclusions about the meaning of vocation?

CHAPTER 2   *What Does My Faith Tell Me about Vocation?*

One morning, during the year I turned forty, I woke up and said to my wife, "I think I need to make a change in my life. I think I need to do something different. Other people change careers. Why can't I?"

I should mention that, by this time in my life, I had been pastor of three Presbyterian churches in three states and had enjoyed my work — mostly. As with any kind of work, parish ministry has its annoying features. Having to work most holidays and weekends, plus a lot of evenings, would be one.

Those annoyances, however, weren't the problem for me on that particular morning. Instead, I had the feeling that maybe, just maybe, there was something else for me to do with my life. I wasn't sure what that "something else" might be, but I wanted to look around and see what else was out there. In the course of my work, I encourage other people to make changes. Sometimes I *challenge* them. So, why shouldn't I do it too?

The risky part, for me, and the reason I couldn't simply act on my feelings that morning, was that I was married with two children who were rapidly approaching college age. Beyond that, I owned a house and had mortgage payments to make. Starting a career when I was in my mid-twenties was easy. Although it didn't always seem that way at the time, I now realize how simple it was. But now things were different: I had other people to consider, serious financial commitments to honor, and a solid track record in a single career path.

Facing the Challenge

I'll get back to my own story in a minute. But first I want to point something out.

I'm well aware that some people are very happy — or at least content — with their lives. Some people, I've noticed, find meaning and purpose in just about everything they do. They never wake up and wonder, as I did, if they should be doing something different with their lives.

Do you know something? I'm happy for them. I really am. To be honest, I enjoy their company. But there aren't very many of them — at least that's the impression I have. Most of the people I talk to in the course of my work tell me that they feel stuck — either in their jobs or, more generally, in their lives. They occasionally describe a place that feels hopeless and desperate, like a deep rut they can't seem to climb out of.

People who feel stuck in life can sometimes keep going for a fairly long time, longer than you might expect. Out of a sense of duty to their families, maybe, or simply out of inertia, they stay where they are and keep doing the same things they've always done. Not happily, not with a sense of purpose or meaning, but they keep doing it.

And then, typically, something happens — usually something big.

In my own case, I would say that what happened wasn't that big. But most other people hit a major bump in life's road. They lose their job, or they get divorced, or they lose a family member. Just about

11

anything in life will do it, any serious jolt or tremor, if they already feel discontented or unhappy with what they're doing.

Recently a fifty-six-year-old man in my church died very suddenly, without warning. Faced with the loss of financial security, his wife found herself in the painful position of having to reassess her life. I was sitting in her living room when she told me that she really didn't like her current part-time job and that it didn't pay much — certainly not enough to live on. But, she said, it had been convenient: good hours, a short distance from home.

> Vocation does not mean a goal that I pursue. It means a calling that I hear. Before I can tell my life what I want to do with it, I must listen to my life telling me who I am. I must listen for the truths and values at the heart of my identity, not the standards by which I must live — but the standards by which I cannot help but live if I am living my own life.
>
> Parker J. Palmer, *Let Your Life Speak: Listening for the Voice of Vocation*

"Now," she told me, "I not only have to find a new job. I have to figure out who I am and what I have to offer, which may be the hard part."

I promised that I and her friends in the church would walk with her during this difficult time in her life, but I remember thinking, "You're in for the challenge of a lifetime."

Remembering the Call

Ten years ago, on the morning I told my wife that I thought I needed to do "something else" with my life, she did something that at the time I found very irritating.

She said, "Okay, if that's what you think you need to do."

What I had half-expected, half-wanted, was this: "Oh, Doug, you can't. Our lives are so good and so stable just the way they are. Please don't do anything that would upset what we've worked so hard to achieve." If that had been her response, you see, I could have gone to work that morning and silently resented her. In other words, I could have blamed her for all of my unhappiness. And that might have been the end of it, as it is for many unhappy people.

Instead, what my wife said was something truly grace-filled. And the irritating part, I quickly realized, was that the ball was now back in my court. I had raised the issue, and she had given me the gift of allowing me to sort it out for myself.

That same day, armed with grace, I made an appointment with a person who talks to a lot of pastors asking the same kinds of questions I had. First this professional put me through the usual battery of personality tests, most of which I had taken years before, as part of the process leading to ordination in the Presbyterian church. Not surprisingly, most of the test results were similar to what they had been before. My hair may have been graying, but my personality hadn't changed much, which was reassuring.

Next I was asked to write a short essay about what I (not others) thought were the major accomplishments of my life up until that point. This assignment was a little more difficult than answering the multiple-choice questions on the personality tests, but I found it helpful and revealing. I surprised myself, and I recommend the exercise to others. It's a good one.

My final assignment was to talk to the professional about my feelings of wanting to do something different with my life. "Some days," I told him, "I feel like little more than the executive director of a nonprofit. I raise money, I encourage a staff, and I worry about lots of inconsequential matters."

"Such as?" he asked.

"Parking," I answered. "When I first signed up for this job, I wanted to do ministry. I wanted to make a difference in people's lives. And what I find myself doing instead is listening to people tell me how hard it is to find a parking place on Sunday morning."

A good listener, the professional was mostly quiet during my whining. Which is all it was, of course. Once or twice he asked a clarifying question, probably so that I would know he was still listening. Finally he leaned forward in his seat and looked both thoughtful and concerned, exactly what you would want in a concerned friend.

"Hmmmmm," he said. "Sounds like you want to get back to whatever it was you originally felt called to do."

And there it was — that little expression I myself have used so often over the years. *Felt called.* What I was hoping for, in a way, was that he would give me an exercise to take home, five practical steps toward contentment and happiness in my life, a career makeover kit: "Tomorrow, Doug, I want you to get going on step one, which is . . ." Instead, what he gave me was a question, something for me to think about: What was it that I *felt called* to do with my life?

I want to ask *you* the same question: What is it that you feel called to do with your life? What is your vocation? Do you know? You might be surprised to learn that you have a vocation, but you do. You've been called to do something with your life, something that will give your life purpose and meaning.

Where Is Galilee in Your Life?

One Easter morning not long ago, I preached a sermon on Matthew's account of the resurrection. Over the years I'm sure I've preached about that story at least half a dozen times, but up until then I had never noticed something obvious in the story — the number of times the little word "go" is used.

In the space of just a few hours, several people visit the empty tomb, and each time the instruction they hear is basically the same: "Come see, and then go." Even Jesus gets into the act. "Don't be afraid," he tells the women who come. "Go — and tell my brothers to get going to Galilee, where I will meet them." Go, go, go.

The repetition has an effect. The people in the story are stunned, amazed, saddened, overjoyed — in other words, their feelings are all over the place — but always there is this command to get moving. Don't stand still, the story seems to say. Get out of here. Beat it. There's work to be done.

In my sermon I happened to mention a Gallup poll that was conducted among college students a few years ago. They were asked to name their primary concern in life, and by far the majority of them said it was the vocational issue.

Not really surprised by that, the researchers decided to ask people of other ages what they were concerned about, and this time they *were* surprised by the results. No matter what their age — whether young, middle-aged, or older — the respondents' number-one concern was essentially the same: What am I supposed to do with my life?

My sermon that Easter morning got some people talking — to me, to their family members, and in some cases, from what I've heard, to their therapists. "I hear Jesus telling me to 'go,'" they would say to me, "but I'm not sure where I'm supposed to be going. What does Galilee look like in my life?"

That's a very fine question — a *vocational* question.

I don't think I fully realized it at the time, but this was one of the best possible outcomes of preaching. My sermon had provided a nudge, perhaps even more, in some journeys of faith.

Let me ask you the question: What does Galilee look like in *your* life? Where is it God wants *you* to go?

The Scope of Vocation

Some Christian traditions — maybe you've noticed — focus on getting people saved. The main question they ask, or so it seems, has to do with your eternal destination. But it has always seemed to me that my faith tradition is better known for something different, something more immediate. My faith tradition, the one in which I was raised, has always seemed to pay a lot more attention to what happens *after* you're saved.

What's supposed to happen after you're saved, I learned, is that you begin to live differently, gratefully, with a brand-new sense of meaning and purpose. And it's then, I was told, that you're pursuing your calling or vocation in life — in other words, what God saved you for. Your life has been altered and claimed and redirected. You're not living for yourself anymore; you're living for the God who loves you and, in a sense, *needs* you. God expects to work through you. God's work will be accomplished — in part — *through you.* (I'll be exploring this idea more fully in the last chapter of this book, where I talk about our being co-creators with God.)

For most of church history, vocation was thought to be what people in religious orders did with their lives. If you became a priest or joined the Benedictines, for example, you had a vocation. But not if you were a farmer. Or a teacher. Or anything else. Vocation was something that was reserved for religious professionals.

But church reformers like Martin Luther and John Calvin emerged in the sixteenth century and took a very different view of work and the way we live our lives. What they did was broaden the meaning of vocation to include virtually all of life. Nearly everything we do with our lives, they said, can be thought of as vocation, as a response to God's claim on our lives.

Think of that. *Everything* we do. Everything we are. Vocation turns out to be a far bigger, far more encompassing concept than most people realize.

IN THE CHAPTERS that follow, I'll focus much of my attention on the part of our lives having to do with jobs or careers. I need to acknowledge that now. Vocation is far more than work, but work — for most of us — is what we do with the majority of our waking hours.

It's important to remember, though, that Luther and Calvin went well beyond work when they wrote about vocation.

Are you thinking about getting married? Well, they said, think about your decision as a calling. Maybe you're called to be married and have the gifts for it. But maybe you're not. Maybe, they said (actually the Apostle Paul makes the case in 1 Corinthians 7), your call in life is not to marriage at all but to singleness. Maybe your gifts make you uniquely suited for that life. If so,

Life develops new purpose, value, and significance as we discover and share our mission. Life is more than a job. Our identity is not in a job. Jobs come and go, wither and fade. We may have several in the course of our lives. Our identity is not in some institution or business. That way of achieving identity no longer works. It is an illusion. The meaning of life is in the mission.

Kennon L. Callahan, *Twelve Keys for Living: Possibilities for a Whole, Healthy Life*

then be the best single person you can possibly be. Honor God with your singleness. Or if you really do feel called to be married, honor God with your marriage. Be the best married person you can possibly be. Either way, think of your life as a vocation.

Are you a son or a daughter? Think of your relationship with your parents as a calling. You can honor God, they said, by being an outstanding son or daughter.

According to Luther and Calvin, these callings are every bit as honorable and important to God as the calling to the priesthood. This was the spiritual breakthrough they achieved — that vocation is all that we are, all that we do.

At the time, this was considered a novel, even radical thought. And in many ways, it still is.

Older Adults and Vocation

People who lived at the time of Luther and Calvin obviously didn't think about retirement because life expectancies were relatively short, and retirement simply wasn't an option. But today, life expectancies are much longer, so asking vocational questions about retirement is important — in fact, I plan to do just that in a later chapter. I'm not aware that very many people are thinking about retirement in vocational terms, so maybe the time has come to start the conversation with some tough questions.

Here are a few: What does God call us to do with our lives after we retire? Is a life of leisure a fitting response to the call of God in our lives? If you're a person of faith, what would be a God-honoring way to retire?

Over the years, because of my work as a pastor, I've spent a great deal of time with older adults. I enjoy them, and I learn from them. (Soon I'll be one of them myself.) What I often find striking is how true the findings of that Gallup poll are: older adults struggle with the issues of meaning, purpose, happiness, and contentment in life as much as any other age group.

And there are older adults who have become models of what I (in a later chapter) call vocational integrity. James Fowler is a scholar who writes about faith development issues, and in his book entitled *Becoming Adult, Becoming Christian,* he says, "There is an impressive quality of dignity, courage, and energy in the lives of those older adults who have found and been faithful to purposes for their lives that are part of the purposes of God."

Baby Boomers and Vocation

If you noted my age at the beginning of this chapter, you might guess that I'm a baby boomer. And you'd be right. I write these words as a boomer, as someone who is keenly aware of midlife issues. Like other people my age, I never expected to be this old.

We baby boomers thought we'd always be young. Maybe every generation assumes that, but boomers in particular grew up with an obsession with youth. We celebrated it, we worshiped it, and at times we rubbed our parents' noses in it. We were people who weren't going to trust anyone over thirty. Remember? It's painful to recall, but true. Now we're so far past thirty we can hardly see it in the rearview mirror.

One newspaper article I saw recently described boomers as "has-beens." That was hard to read. With the burst of the stock-market bubble in 2000, many of those who lost their jobs were — for the first time — baby boomers. Numerous businesses were downsized, and many of us were let go to make room for a generation of younger, less expensive, and in some cases better trained and educated workers. Many of us may even be wondering if our best days and our greatest achievements are behind us.

A member of the church I served previously was forty-five years old when the telecommunications industry fell on hard times. She lost what had been a good job — good salary, benefits, and title. She told me that to get severance benefits she was required to sign a release promising not to sue for age discrimination. "That's when it hit me," she said. "I'm old." And job searching has led her into a period of extended soul searching.

For the first time in her life, she says that she's seriously considering work in the nonprofit world — partly because she needs to be flexible, but mostly because her goals have changed. For her, as for many others, midlife has been a time to reconsider, re-evaluate, and refocus.

I was sorry, of course, that my friend lost her job. It was a situation I wouldn't wish on anyone. But I can truthfully say that I've enjoyed the conversations we've had as a result — both about her job searching and about her soul searching. Midlife brings with it —

sometimes unexpectedly — a great deal of vocational struggle. James Fowler says that people at midlife are usually "prime candidates for a major encounter with vocational clarification."

I like that term. "Vocational clarification" nicely summarizes the vocational task for most people at midlife.

Young Adults and Vocation

Older adults and those at midlife aren't the only ones who ask questions about meaning and purpose in life. Young adults do too.

I have an unusually large number of nieces and nephews, and I'm grateful for all of them. I enjoy the time I spend with them, and I enjoy being their uncle. Part of that relationship, of course, is watching them grow up. And in the last few years, as they've started making their way through college and thinking about life after college, our conversations have turned to vocation.

Older adults may think that young adulthood is fun and carefree, but often it's not. Often the years of young adulthood are difficult, stressful, even frightening. At our holiday get-togethers, the conversation almost inevitably rolls around to school and work. "So, what's your major?" "What do you think you're going to do after college?" "Got any jobs lined up after June?"

> A true calling reveals its presence by the enjoyment and sense of renewed energies its practice yields us. This does not mean that sometimes we do not groan inwardly at the weight of the burdens imposed on us or that we never feel reluctance about re-entering bloody combat. Indeed, there are times when we wish we did not have to face every burden our calling imposes on us. Still, finding ourselves where we are and with the responsibilities we bear, we know it is our duty — part of what we are meant to do — to soldier on.
>
> Michael Novak,
> *Business as a Calling*

Early on, I found myself wanting to tell my nieces and nephews what I thought they should do with their lives. But I soon learned that my advice wasn't particularly helpful — usually it wasn't even wanted. What I needed to do, I discovered, was to be available, to answer when asked specific questions, and to pray a great deal, right along with their parents. I now think the best possible thing an uncle (or aunt or any other family member) can do is to walk alongside these young people as they answer their vocational questions for themselves.

Trumpets in the Morning

When I graduated from seminary — a long time ago — the commencement speaker was a man named W. Frank Harrington. He has since died, but at the time he was the pastor of the largest Presbyterian church in the country and someone my classmates and I respected and admired.

One of his statements that day — it may have been part of the title of his speech — has stayed with me over the years. He was speaking about his zest for life and his passion for his work, and he said, "As far as I'm concerned, I still hear trumpets in the morning!"

I remember thinking, "Wow, what a way to wake up!"

It would be wonderful, wouldn't it, to feel this way. Imagine it — waking up every morning as though you're being summoned to something important, feeling as though your work is critical to the well-being of others, feeling as though there's such meaning and purpose in your life that you can't wait to start your day.

I've always wanted that feeling for myself. In reality, though, I only hear trumpets on some mornings. And some people, I realize, never hear them at all.

But I'm convinced that more of us would hear trumpets more of the time if we began to think of our lives differently — as a vocation, as a response to the call of God in our lives.

THE STORY I started this chapter with — the one about my relatively brief, midlife vocational crisis — has a happy ending. As I drove home after my last meeting with the professional who led me through all of the personality tests and conversations about what I really felt called to do with my life, an unexpected thought occurred to me: "I'm already doing it."

What I'm supposed to be doing with my life, that is. I'd been doing it for a long, long time, as a matter of fact.

After all of the questions and tests and conversations, I ended up right back where I started. I ended up by reclaiming my vocation, my sense of calling. Ministry, I came to see, makes use of my gifts in a way that no other way of life possibly could. I suddenly felt as though my call had been confirmed, or reaffirmed, which came as both a wonderful relief and the starting point for renewed enthusiasm about my work.

How about you? Do you know what you're supposed to be doing with your life?

QUESTIONS FOR REFLECTION AND DISCUSSION

1. What's the first thing that comes to your mind when you hear the word "call" or "vocation"? Is it going to require an adjustment for you to broaden your thinking about what a call might mean?

2. Martin Luther and John Calvin revolutionized our thinking about vocation by including not only our jobs but also (among other things) our marriages and our family relationships. Can you think of other areas of life that have — or could have — the characteristics of a call? How would those areas be different if you began to think of them in terms of vocation?

3. To have a sense of meaning and purpose in life sometimes means the feeling of being summoned to a place or a situation where you're needed. Where are the places in your life where you feel summoned?

✒ CHAPTER 3   *How Do I Find Meaning and Purpose?*

A couple of summers ago I was on vacation with my family at our favorite vacation spot on Lake Michigan. What I ordinarily like to do during this time is sit on my beach chair and read books for two weeks — and not much else. Some of the books I read turn out to be helpful for my work, but many are just for fun. I've found that reading on the beach is just the right sort of replenishing break I need in my life. Occasionally I'll get up and cool off in the lake, but then it's back to the chair and the books.

One day as I was heading back to my chair after a swim, I saw someone walking along the shoreline, someone I've known for a long time. So I went over to say hello.

When she saw me, she said hello and asked if the girls sunbathing near my chair were my daughters. When I said yes, she said, "Oh, they're so lovely." And when I said, "Aren't they, though," she added, quite unexpectedly, "And they have their *whole lives* in front of them."

Looking back on this exchange, I realize that I knew almost immediately that this was a comment begging for deeper attention. After all, I've known this person for a long time, and so at some level I knew she was expressing regret. I could feel it. I know the sound of regret when I hear it. And, beyond that, I thought I saw a look of wistfulness in her eyes as she looked over at my daughters.

But instead of responding to the regret, I deflected it. I didn't want to deal with it at that particular moment. I was on vacation, after all, and I didn't want to do what I usually do in those situations. Beyond that, I've known the pain of regret in my own life, and, quite frankly, I didn't feel like ruining a perfectly good day at the beach by getting in touch with some pain from my past.

So I blurted out something like, "Oh, you have *over half* of your life to look forward to." I said it with a wink and a smile, hoping she'd sense some gentle teasing about her age. But at the same time, I knew I was capable of a far better pastoral response than that.

Later in the day I thought about my conversation with this old friend, and I scolded myself for missing an opportunity to express compassion and concern. This woman is in her early forties, and she has three young boys. At some point earlier in her life, she had made what for her was a difficult and life-altering decision not to be a public school teacher anymore. She taught briefly, did it well, and was well regarded by her students. But after careful consideration she decided she needed to be home in the role of a full-time mom.

From all appearances, she's doing a terrific job at it. I wouldn't call her boys "lovely," but they're certainly what our culture would consider to be the masculine counterpart of that. Still, I happen to know — through friends, mostly — that she's struggling on several levels of her life, in her marriage and in her personal life too. So her comment about my girls having their "whole lives" to look forward to seemed to be an expression of regret, a glimpse into her own sense of worth, and a question about the choices she had made some years ago.

That little conversation obviously got under my skin. I had already decided at that point to write a book about vocation, and much of my vacation reading was focused on the subject of vocation, so naturally I heard her comments through the filter, you might say, of this subject. And there was something about what she said that was not only poignant but very much to the point. She expressed something that I hear a great deal during the course of my pastoral work, and often from people her age — or, more accurately, people *my* age. She was questioning the choices she had made earlier in her life — and living with regret.

Life Stages

I'm convinced that life stages play a crucial role in our understanding of vocation. Where we are in life — young adulthood, midlife, or older adulthood — profoundly affects the way we think about vocation. But I've also come to see that the underlying search is basically the same no matter what our age.

Here's the same thought in different words. Life stage is an important factor to consider when talking about vocation. It affects the *circumstances* of our vocation and — to some degree — our range of options. In this chapter, in fact, I want to explore a little of what happens to us at different life stages. But the search itself, finding our vocation in life, is the same, no matter how old we are.

Whether we're twenty or eighty, we want our lives to have purpose and meaning.

Young Adulthood   My memory is dimming, but I do remember a few things from my young adult years. And to tell the truth, I have basically fond memories of that time in my life. Today my work brings me into contact with quite a few young adults, which is a satisfying part of what I do, and together we talk about the issues that they face. Beyond that, as I mentioned in the last chapter, I've been blessed with a large number of nieces and nephews, most of whom are in this particular life stage now.

I'll make this claim, then, with confidence: The young adults I've known over the years, those people who are heading into their twenties, typically wonder a great deal about what they're supposed to do with their lives.

Very few young adults know from an early age what they're going to do. Some do, but most don't. In my experience, the majority of young adults consider a variety of options, and some even experience a false start or two along the way. (My own perspective on false starts is that they can be deeply valuable in the process of finding our vocation, but to young adults — not surprisingly — they feel like wasted time in the push to get started with life. I'll say more about this in a later chapter.)

The sheer number of choices available to most young adults can feel overwhelming. And that may be the single biggest vocational issue that they face. Temptations also loom large — in fact, that may be the next biggest vocational issue for young adults. After all, some mistakes do have lasting effects on our lives.

For these reasons and others, the transition into young adulthood can be — and often is — one of the most difficult periods of life.

The good news is that many young adults have grown up believing that they are uniquely equipped to do something special with their lives, that they've been called to something. They've been asked from an early age, for example, what they plan to do when they grow up, and they've been coached, mentored, helped, and sometimes prodded — usually by their parents — to seek out a path that feels right to them.

But how do they decide which path is right? If you're a young adult, how do *you* decide? (Maybe you picked up this book hoping that I'd tell you, and I do have some suggestions for you in the next chapter.) How can you know at twenty-five what you'll enjoy doing at forty-five? Or what you'll find satisfying at sixty-five?

The truthful answer is, you can't. Life doesn't work that way. You won't know at twenty-five. But you'll be working your way toward knowing.

One of the reasons that college students change their majors as often as they do (two to three times on average) is that they're struggling to find the path that feels right. Young adulthood involves many issues, but no more important issue than sorting and sifting through the many options that life presents.

Midlife   Midlife issues, as I'm now keenly aware, are no less real and no less stressful than those of young adulthood. (If you're a young adult, you probably didn't want to hear that. But you need to know it.)

What most people at midlife experience, I think, is a narrowing of options. If the most daunting prospect at twenty-five is too many choices, then the most daunting prospect at forty-five is recognizing how limited those choices have become. The choices I made at twenty-five, it's now very clear, have profoundly affected the range of options I have at midlife. I simply can't do certain things now because of choices that I made back then.

Some of those earlier decisions were good ones, and I'm proud of them. But others weren't so good. And regrettably, I can't turn back the clock to change them.

When this book was at a very early stage, a dear friend challenged me on this issue. She said, "Maybe for men the range of options narrows, but for women, especially those who've stayed home to care for kids, the world begins to open up again at midlife."

> The human calling . . . is to undergo and participate in the widening inclusiveness of the circle of those who count as neighbor, from the narrowness of our familial beginnings toward real solidarity with a commonwealth of being. This calling means movement from the limiting love of those who love us and on whom we are dependent toward the limitless love that comes from genuine identification with the source and center of all being.
>
> James W. Fowler,
> *Becoming Adult, Becoming Christian: Adult Development and Christian Faith*

I sense the wisdom in what she said. It seems obvious to me that men and women have different views on vocational matters. The gender roles that we've been assigned by family, church, and culture are enormous factors in the search for vocation. So I have no doubt that many women view midlife differently than men do.

On the other hand, I'm not prepared to give up my point — at least not entirely. By the time you reach your forties — whether you're a man or a woman — your options have narrowed. If I were to enter law school today, my chances of becoming a Supreme Court Justice would be remote. And that would be equally true for anyone else my age, male or female. We simply can't hope to achieve all the goals that may have been realistic for us to pursue earlier in our lives.

One of the career options I considered when I was in college was journalism. I loved to write, and I loved being around newspapers. I really thought, for a while, that the publishing business was in my future.

Since I've been away from it, however, the technology alone has changed so much that the newspaper business is almost unrecognizable to me today. The pace of change has been breathtaking, and so many of the skills I developed by working on the college paper simply aren't needed anymore. This is one door, among many, that now seems closed to me at midlife. It would be unrealistic to think that I could somehow get back into journalism, at least in the way I used to think about it.

And I think this is what most of us in midlife discover — that we have far fewer career choices than we once had.

I had a cup of coffee with a member of my last church who, like me, is in midlife. For twenty years he was a stock trader and analyst. From everything he's accumulated, I would say he made a good living at it too. But when the stock bubble burst in 2000, he lost his job and had no success in finding a new one. His skills are still valued by some companies, but investment firms today are more likely to hire recent college graduates.

But my friend has always been good with tools, so he's currently making a living (a much more modest one) doing home remodeling. As he put it, he's having to "reinvent" himself — one of the most difficult challenges he's ever had to face. My own sense is that he's still on a vocational journey. But for practical reasons he now finds himself doing something he never expected to be doing at this point in his life.

It's true that, for some, midlife can be a time of new freedom and new opportunity. But for many — including me — it's a time of letting go, of giving up old dreams. It's a time for accepting with grace (and humor) the choices that were made long ago, and then moving on.

Older Adulthood   Older adults, I now realize, have just as many stresses, problems, and challenges as younger people.

It's funny how I once thought they didn't. I assumed that, at a certain age, most of the really pressing issues in life would be largely resolved. It turns out I was wrong about that. I certainly wasn't aware of it when I was growing up, but I now realize that Grandma and Grandpa were probably a lot more stressed out than I ever imagined.

One question I hear from older adults is this: "What now? The losses are piling up fast, physical as well as emotional. How do I find purpose and meaning at this point in my life?" That's a vocational question, of course, but in older adulthood it's asked differently. The fear is that purpose and meaning may no be longer available or possible.

When my grandmother reached her mid-nineties, she regularly expressed the feeling that she was "ready to go," that she had outlived her usefulness. Though that was difficult to hear at the time, I now understand a little better what she was saying. She very much *wanted* her life to have purpose and meaning, and when she felt it no longer could or would, she was ready to let go of it.

But, on the positive side, I've noticed that many older adults do reach a point in their lives where they feel a remarkable sense of confidence in who they are. As they do the work of reflecting and remembering, they see (finally) how the various strands of their lives fit together. Regrets typically give way to acceptance. It's a delightful experience to be in the presence of older adults who have reached this point.

The Search for Meaning

Whatever our stage in life, I think we're always searching for meaning. It's critical to our well-being, to our very sense of self.

Viktor Frankl made this argument in a very compelling way. As a Holocaust survivor who was also a psychiatrist, he wrote *Man's Search for Meaning*, a riveting account of his years in Nazi death camps. The horror he endured is unimaginable but real. His entire family — father, mother, brother, and wife — perished in the camps, and he, like all of the other prisoners, lost everything that had been of value to him.

Because of his training, he couldn't help but make clinical observations about the prisoners around him, as well as about his own thoughts and feelings. And in the book he comes to a clear and unambiguous conclusion about why some in the camps survived while others did not. As he observed the prisoners around him, he would sometimes witness the exact moment when the will to endure, the sense of fundamental meaning, disappeared. And when that was gone, death soon followed.

The opposite of meaning, Frankl concluded, was despair. "Woe to him," he writes, "who saw no more sense to his life, no aim, no purpose, and therefore no point in carrying on. He was soon lost."

Years later, in his work with patients, Frankl would sometimes ask those in particularly dark circumstances, "Why don't you commit suicide?" It's certainly a startling question, but there was a therapeutic purpose behind it. From the answers that his patients gave him, Frankl writes, he was able to shape the course of their therapy. Sometimes it was a love for his children, and no more, that kept a patient from ending his life. Other times it was a talent or a special gift. And

> Those who have a "why" to live can bear with almost any "how."
>
> Viktor Frankl

still other times it was merely a desire to keep certain memories alive. Whatever it was, it would become the basis on which to build a life, a life with meaning.

Frankl's entire approach to his work was built on his experiences in the death camps, and so he sharply disagreed with his mentor, Sigmund Freud, who argued that the basic impulse in life is for pleasure. Frankl's experiences pointed him in a much different direction. He believed that meaning, not pleasure, was what we human beings crave more than anything else.

And on that point I find myself in agreement with him. Our search for vocation is ultimately a search for meaning and purpose in our lives.

ABRAHAM MASLOW was one of the most influential psychologists of the last century. He observed and studied a few of the highly productive and successful people in his life and concluded that some people, a very small percentage, enjoy a greater degree of psychological health and maturity than most. He called these people "self-actualized."

Maslow's views, it's important to note, have come under criticism recently, especially by feminist scholars, who note that almost all of his examples of self-actualized people are men. Still, there are a number of enduring insights in Maslow's work.

According to Maslow, self-actualized people possess creativity, spontaneity, flexibility, and humility, among other characteristics. In addition, Maslow observed, they are dedicated to some work, task, duty, or vocation. They are so dedicated, in fact, that for them the usual distinction between work and play is blurred. Work itself is pleasurable for them because it provides meaning and purpose.

YOU WON'T BE surprised when I say that the issue here is fundamentally a spiritual one. When people talk about finding purpose and meaning in their lives — or for that matter, when they talk about finding happiness and contentment — I hear them describing what is essentially a spiritual longing.

If people express regret over a decision they made in the past, like my friend at the beach, if they wonder about choices they made long ago and how those choices affect their lives today, or if they wonder whether life itself is worth living, they are raising *spiritual* issues.

The faith I embrace, the tradition in which I've been raised, has something profound to say about these issues. My faith tradition, as I pointed out in the last chapter, has been addressing these issues, and others like them, down through the centuries.

What I believe — and at some level I think I've been aware of this my whole life — is that God has something in mind for each of us. God calls us — not simply to careers, though that's part of it. God calls us not only to do but to *be* something with our lives. And we find purpose and meaning in life when we become the people we were created to be, when we respond to and grow into our calling. To find purpose and meaning — even happiness and contentment — in life, spiritually speaking, is always going to be about identifying God's will or plan for us.

Another way of saying that is this: until we find ourselves in sync with or in alignment with God's call, we're going to be restless, unfulfilled, discontented, and difficult. People who struggle vocationally, people who struggle with what they're supposed to be doing with their lives, can be difficult to live with.

So, if you're not doing this for yourself, then please do it for those who are close to you. Figure out what God has in mind for you. If you've been called to do or be something with your life, then your sense of purpose and meaning will become clear as you do it. To paraphrase the Apostle Paul's words in Romans 12: If you're a preacher,

32

preach! If you're a helper, help! If you're a teacher, teach! If you give guidance, then do it! And do it cheerfully.

A Life of Service

How do you find out what God has in mind for you to do with your life?

That's the big question, isn't it? Or it's *one* of the big questions. I have more to say about it in the next chapter. Discernment — figuring things out — is a critically important process in finding our vocation. For now I'll just say that recognizing our gifts and learning to see ourselves as we really are would be two important steps in finding God's call for us.

Before I say any more about that, however, I challenge you to consider a life of service. If you want to find a life full of purpose and meaning, more purpose and more meaning than you can possibly imagine, consider a life in which you offer yourself in service to others.

To me this is the single biggest contribution that Christian faith can make to any conversation about vocation. For Jewish people in the first century, keeping the law was the way to find purpose and meaning in life. Keeping the law, they believed, was itself fulfilling and life-giving. So, in a story told in Matthew's Gospel, Jesus is asked to name the greatest commandment of them all. The question contained a trap, of course (because *all* of the commandments are important), but Jesus neatly sidestepped it by saying, in effect, "Love God and love others."

And one of them, a lawyer, asked him a question to test him. "Teacher, which commandment in the law is the greatest?" He said to him, " 'You shall love the Lord your God with all your heart, and with all your soul, and with all your mind.' This is the greatest and first commandment. And a second is like it: 'You shall love your neighbor as yourself.' "

Matthew 22:35-39, NRSV

In a sense that's all any of us really need to know about vocation.

Whatever your gifts turn out to be, whatever your particular aptitudes in life are, whatever you happen to be really good at, whatever life stage you're in — your deepest feelings of fulfillment will occur when you're giving yourself away, when you're living a life of service, when you find a way to use your gifts and aptitudes — as Jesus once put it — to love your neighbor as yourself.

I LIKE this story. A traveler was making his way through Europe as the great cathedrals were being built, and one day he met three workers. He asked the first one, "What are you doing?"

The worker replied, "I'm cutting stone."

Later the traveler put the same question to the next worker he met: "What are you doing?"

The next worker answered, "I'm cutting stone so that I can provide for my family."

Finally, later in the day, the traveler put the question to the third worker he met, also a stone cutter. "What are you doing?" he asked.

According to the story, the third worker beamed, as if relishing the thought. He answered, "I'm building a great cathedral!"

We all know people like the first two workers — those who are focused on the task at hand and its immediate benefits. And we all know people like the third worker, who, though they may not be building a great cathedral — or whatever the modern equivalent is — see what they do as part of a larger picture, as part of a larger calling.

The point of telling this story is to underscore how important it is for us to understand that the call is always to something bigger and more important than ourselves. If you're living for yourself and for yourself alone, I can guarantee that you'll have problems. Why? Because, spiritually speaking, it's an empty, shallow, and superficial way to live. On the other hand, if you're giving of yourself, you'll find depth, substance, and ultimately meaning in life.

From the spiritual point of view, that's just the way it works.

I like the way Frederick Buechner puts it in his book *Wishful Thinking*: "The place God calls you to is the place where your deep gladness and the world's deep hunger meet."

Exactly so.

Duty, Obligation, Commitment, Sacrifice

Here's one last point to keep in mind.

I think it's important, in any conversation about vocation, to talk about duty, obligation, commitment, and sacrifice. To be called to something implies these words and others like them. I don't see how you can claim to have a call from God without the sense of being compelled by it.

These four nouns, I'm sorry to say, have become almost foreign words to us. Unwelcome words. We hear them, but we don't necessarily like them. We fear what they might ask of us. But I think we should hear them more often. Most of the people I've known over the years, people who live their lives with a strong sense of purpose and meaning, have also had an obvious sense of duty, obligation, commitment, and sacrifice. And so I think there's a connection here that we should explore.

I'm aware that there may be unhealthy dimensions to duty, obligation, commitment, and sacrifice, but it seems to me that our culture is almost too focused on those negatives. I would like us to re-examine what those words might mean for us. Not every duty, after all, is bad, not every obligation is unhealthy, not every commitment is oppressive. And sometimes sacrifice builds and enriches our character in wonderful ways.

> For you were called to freedom, brothers and sisters; only do not use your freedom as an opportunity for self-indulgence, but through love become slaves to one another.
>
> Galatians 5:13, NRSV

Many of us were raised to value freedom — and personal freedom in particular. And while we can be grateful for the freedoms we've known, I wonder if it's not time for some of us to focus on other dimensions of life. Living a life of service is going to require something from us, perhaps focusing less on ourselves and paying more attention to the people around us. If we begin to do that, if we begin to live our lives with a sense of service, we will experience far more satisfaction with our lives, far more pride in what we do, far more meaning in our work.

And far less regret.

What would happen if you were to begin each day by asking yourself this question: "I wonder what duty or responsibility God is placing before me today?"

QUESTIONS FOR REFLECTION AND DISCUSSION

1. Assess your life stage, and then ask yourself this question: What are the options that are open to me? Do they seem overwhelming? Narrowing? Or few and far between? What could I realistically accomplish at this point in my life?

2. Based on his prison-camp experiences, Viktor Frankl argues that the desire for meaning is the deepest human desire we have. Do you agree? What would you say a human being longs for more than anything else?

3. What are the healthy kinds of duty, obligation, sacrifice, and service that you have in your life? If you experience unhealthy kinds of duty, obligation, sacrifice, or service, how might you be able to change that?

 **CHAPTER 4**   *How Do I Discern*
God's Call?

W hen the subject of vocation comes up, one of the first questions people ask is, "How do you know?" If each of us is called
by God to do or to be something special with our lives, how do we determine what it is?

Some people seem to have no problem whatsoever figuring out
what to do with their lives. And there are even people who will say
that they "always knew" that they would grow up to be a rock star or a
basketball player or a teacher. In other words, their vocation seemed
clear from an early age.

That wasn't the way it was for me, and if you're reading this book,
I'm guessing that it probably isn't that way for you now. My sense is
that the vast majority of us have to go through a process of discernment, of careful listening for God's call in our lives, and that's what
this chapter is about: listening for God's call.

The Example of Moses

Since childhood, one of my favorite Bible stories has been the call of Moses at the burning bush. Over the years the story has been the source of many, many sermons, including the first sermon I preached in front of a "live" congregation — not just a room full of seminary classmates.

Each time I've come back to the story over the years, I've seen something new in it. When I reread the story recently, I was struck by how well-equipped and uniquely suited Moses was to lead the people out of Egypt — and how Moses himself couldn't see it. In fact, how he at first *refused* to see it.

According to the story (and I encourage you to reread it if it's been a while since you've spent time with it), Moses grew up in Pharaoh's household and had access along the way to the very best that Egypt had to offer. Of course, he had no idea at the time that he was being prepared for anything later in his life, so when God calls to him out of the burning bush, he is utterly and completely clueless — and flat-out obstinate. Often in life, I've noticed, the two go together.

On five separate occasions (it's actually a lengthy story), Moses objects and tells God he's not up to the job God has in mind for him. He comes up with a variety of excuses and obstacles. Among other things, he tells God that he's not a public speaker and he's not politically astute. God grows increasingly irritated with Moses' resistance, but in response to each excuse God promises Moses that he will receive everything he needs.

And maybe that's the *first lesson* about vocation to notice in the story: God matches our cluelessness — and obstinance — with persistence. *If God is calling us to do something (and we're not listening), it's not likely that God will just give up and go away.*

God was determined to have Moses, and God is determined to have us.

I've always taken that to be good news, by the way, because no matter how far I happen to wander from what God has in mind for me, I've always assumed that God will eventually guide me back to where I need to be.

As a matter of fact, maybe a certain amount of resistance, saying no, isn't such a bad thing.

I know this may sound like strange advice, especially coming from a pastor, but stay with me here. If God is determined to have us, if God won't take no for an answer, then maybe one way to test a call, one way to find out if the call is of God, is simply to be patient and not rush into anything.

For most of us, what harm would there be in moving slowly and making sure the voice we're hearing is God's?

HERE'S A *second lesson* to take away from the story: *God not only calls us but equips us.* God has something in mind for each of us to do, and God will give us all the tools and gifts we will ever need to embrace those calls — no matter how far-fetched they may seem to us at the time.

> To get somebody's attention, God always says his name at least twice: "Samuel, Samuel," or "Saul, Saul." The call is not self-evident.
>
> William H. Willimon,
> "Back to the Burning Bush,"
> *Christian Century*

When I first started to explore my call to parish ministry, I was well aware that I, like Moses, dreaded the prospect of public speaking. I like to write, but speaking in front of large groups of people scared the daylights out of me. I couldn't imagine myself as a preacher. For a long time I couldn't do any public speaking without visibly trembling.

Most people are disbelieving when I tell them about this today, but it's true. I was so anxious, so terrified, in front of a group that in college I fulfilled the speech requirement during the summer months, when I figured that fewer of my classmates would be around. As it turned out, I was terribly shaky anyway, but somehow I passed.

Former Duke University pastor (and now Methodist bishop) William Willimon has written a wonderful essay about the call of Moses, and in it he says, "Perhaps God likes a challenge. Maybe a Creator who makes something out of nothing considers vocation a continuing aspect of creation. Any God who could make a man like Moses into a wonderful leader must be some kind of God."

I like to tell myself that any God who could make a public speaker out of me must be really serious about vocation.

Exploring Possibilities

In a helpful book about vocation called *The Fabric of This World,* which is written with college students in mind, philosophy professor Lee Hardy tells how his students over the years have come to him with anguished questions about what to do with their lives after graduation.

Hardy writes a little about the discernment process, about how we're to assess the gifts we've been given and so forth, and then he says something that I find both comforting and reassuring. For most of us, he writes, it's going to take a while to get a fix on what God is saying to us. Listening for God's call in our lives is always going to involve a certain amount of trial and error. Not very many of us get it right the first time.

When I was a college senior, I can remember going to see a guidance counselor on campus and telling him that seminary was a possibility I had considered. I hadn't taken the usual course of study for seminary students (I wasn't a religious studies major), but I confided to him that I had a nagging feeling (that's how it felt) that maybe I should think about ministry. I couldn't get it out of my mind, I told him, even though (God knows) I had tried.

I'll never forget what this person told me that day as he looked at my academic file. What he said, basically, was, "Go ahead. Explore it. Why not? Take a year to see if it's right for you. You'll never know unless you check it out."

So I took his advice. I tried to find out if seminary was for me. It wasn't clear at first, which was okay with me, because deep down I was hoping that I wasn't being called to ministry. But at a certain point in my seminary training — a lot later than you might expect — I discovered what I felt called to do with my life.

I had taken a year off from my studies to complete an internship in a small church in a university town. About halfway through that year, I knew. And not because I was particularly good at being a parish minister. I just knew. Being a pastor of a church was what I felt called to do with my life. And I returned for my last year of seminary preparation with a clarity that I had never had before.

So HOW do we respond to a potential call? It depends in part on our stage of life.

To young adults today I often give the same advice I was given: "Go ahead. Explore it. Why not? See if this feeling you have is genuine. Test it. You'll know soon enough if this path is the right one for you."

To people at midlife, I would say, "You know, the trial-and-error approach is going to be a whole lot riskier at this point in your life. If you sense that God is calling you in a different direction entirely, I would pay attention, but I would also take your time. As you move into midlife, there's more riding on your vocational decisions."

On the other hand, I would add, "But don't put it out of your mind, either." There are ways to find out what God is calling you to do with your life without abruptly quitting your job and moving your family across the country. I don't know how old Moses was when he encountered the burning bush, but he had clearly established a life for himself. He had married, and he had entered his father-in-law's business. He had every reason to move slowly. And he did — at first.

To older adults who sense God's call in their lives, I have said, "There's never going to be a better time in your life to explore!"

One of the consolations of getting older, I think, is that the need to prove ourselves diminishes. So older adults can focus increasingly on other things — less on what will impress other people, and more on what's really important and meaningful.

In addition, older adults, if they're healthy and independent, often have the freedom and opportunity to explore God's call in ways that might not have been possible before. I'm sure there are risks to consider, but that's true at every age.

When I served a church in New Jersey several years ago, a couple told me one day that they felt called to make a significant change in their lives. They were going to sell their home, they told me, and leave for Americus, Georgia, where they would receive training to serve long-term for Habitat for Humanity.

And so, in their early sixties, with their children grown and living on their own, they quit their jobs, left town, developed a brand-new set of skills, learned to speak Spanish fluently, and spent the rest of their lives building homes in Nicaragua.

I hated to see them go, because they were so important to my church. But they left because they firmly believed that this was the time in their lives to do something more, something different, something they had been unable to do earlier in their lives.

My Friend Fred

My favorite story about an unusual vocational path is told by a friend and mentor of mine. For many years Fred Anderson has been the pastor of Madison Avenue Presbyterian Church on the Upper East Side of Manhattan, but the path he took to get there is interesting, to say the least. The people who wander into his church might guess that his path to that historic church was simple and straightforward. It was anything but.

Blessed with a marvelous tenor voice, Fred studied music during his college years and thought for a long time that he was being called to a career in opera. When the Vietnam war was at its height, Fred entered the air force and became an officer and a member of a flight crew stationed in southeast Asia. By the time his military career was over several years later, Fred started to feel the call to ministry, and he enrolled in seminary.

As he likes to tell the story — and he does a far better job of it than I do — God had been preparing him all along. His music training has enabled him to be a leader in giving worship direction to the church. His air-force experience has equipped him to be a superb administrator and staff leader. And of course his seminary training was one of the final pieces of his preparation. His path to ministry wasn't straight, but in hindsight there was a certain logic to it.

> There are all different kinds of voices calling you to all different kinds of work, and the problem is to find out which is the voice of God rather than of Society, say, or the Superego, or Self-Interest. By and large a good rule for finding out is this: The kind of work God usually calls you to is the kind of work (a) that you need most to do and (b) that the world most needs to have done.
>
> Frederick Buechner,
> *Wishful Thinking: A Seeker's ABC*

Whenever he tells the story about his life, Fred likes to say that "nothing is ever wasted," which I've always taken as a valuable spiritual lesson. God is able to use *all* of our experiences — including, as we'll see in a later chapter, the failures and disappointments in our lives — to prepare us for our callings.

HERE'S SOMETHING else to consider.

I sometimes hear people talk about the "false starts" that they've made in their lives. They set out in one direction only to realize that it wasn't for them, and they started over. The terminology they use tends to suggest that there was something negative or wasted about the direction they abandoned.

Maybe it's time to look at these efforts from a vocational perspective. Maybe what we sometimes call "false starts" are in fact necessary first steps, full of good lessons and experiences, for what will come later in our lives. Though it's not always evident at the time, every life experience can teach us a valuable lesson.

Assessing Our Gifts

A first step, if not *the* first step, in discerning God's call in our lives is to undertake an honest assessment of our skills and gifts. College students typically have access to a wide array of tests and personal inventories through guidance offices and on-campus counseling services. I heartily recommend that young adults take advantage of these resources.

At one point in my seminary training I went through a three-day battery of tests and interviews. It's a required process for everyone who's preparing for ordination in the Presbyterian Church today.

I found the process to be very helpful — and at times quite scary. After all, up until that point in my life, I had never really received such a thorough and objective appraisal. But I came away from it knowing myself much better — or at least having the vocabulary to describe my particular gifts. I also began to realize why certain things came easily to me, and why others were always such a chore. For the first time in my life I began to trust my strengths — and find ways to compensate for my weaknesses.

Access to such services seems to diminish with age. Sometimes employers provide outplacement services to workers who are being laid off, and I always encourage the people I know in these situations to take full advantage of them.

Over the years I've encouraged a number of men who were struggling with vocational issues at midlife to seek out career development centers. There's a limit to how much honest evaluation we can do on our own, so feedback from counselors as well as friends and peers can be extraordinarily helpful. Family members and spouses often have a difficult time providing objective evaluations of our gifts. They can be helpful in countless ways, but they sometimes don't see us as we really are.

The truth is, sometimes we don't see *ourselves* as we really are. Sometimes our self-concepts are seriously distorted or flawed. Sometimes the inaccurate messages we received in childhood, from parents or peers, prevent us from seeing our true selves and therefore from achieving our full stature.

Identifying what gets in our way is critical to assessing and using our gifts to their greatest potential, to reaching our true vocation.

Six Stumbling Blocks

If meaning and purpose in life were so easy to achieve, I wouldn't be writing this book. If the people I meet with and talk to during the course of my work could discover their vocations without my help, there would be no need to identify what gets in our way. But clearly there are some things that are stumbling blocks, and I've made a list of them. There may be others, but these are the ones I see most often.

First, as I've already noted, we sometimes face an enormous temptation to prove something, to demonstrate just how capable we are — to parents, friends, spouses, even children. I think the temptation is strongest when we're entering young adulthood. It seems to diminish over time, but it never really goes away.

So, if you're making vocational decisions to impress somebody in your life — or to prove something to yourself — you're headed for trouble. You're going to have a tough time making good decisions.

I'll be honest. This one has been a stumbling block in my own life. For most of my life, if someone said to me, "I don't know, Doug — that may be too tough for you to handle," I was determined to prove them wrong. "Oh, yeah?" I would think. "I'll show you." And most of the time I did. I pushed myself hard — and sometimes in directions that weren't always right for me. I don't think I made any major mistakes, but I certainly could have. And I probably wasted a lot of time and energy in the process. When I'm challenged, I find it very, very difficult to back down. What about you?

My first instinct, by the way, is to say that this is most often a male issue, but I know better. Women like to prove themselves too. So for both men and women, the point is the same: Good vocational decision-making doesn't begin with the need to prove something to somebody else — or to ourselves.

Second, if money is high on your list of considerations as you make your vocational decisions, you're going to regret it sooner or later. Take it from me: no amount of money is going to fill your life with meaning and purpose, joy and fulfillment. It just doesn't work that way. And the earlier in our lives we learn that lesson, the better our lives will be.

Not long ago the alumni magazine from the college I attended ran a series of profiles of recent graduates. The series title, interestingly enough, was "Downwardly mobile, upwardly directed." The magazine offered story after story about graduates who had given up the pursuit of success, as it's defined by popular culture, to live lives of service. Every time I saw one of those profiles I felt a surge of . . . not pride exactly, though I think highly of my college, but something more like affirmation. Only a Christian college, I thought, would dare to lift up life choices like the ones in these profiles and celebrate them. In the current cultural climate, it takes courage to be "downwardly mobile."

One popular approach to career guidance (I hesitate to call it vocational advice) is to say, "Do what you love, and the money will follow." Not putting the pursuit of financial reward first seems wise to me. But there's still the suggestion, isn't there, that we should nevertheless get the reward?

When I worked as a pastor in Illinois, I lived in one of the most affluent counties in the country. The effects of materialism were all around me, and I felt the pressures of it, as did my children. The temptation to make choices based on my perceived need for wealth was sometimes overpoweringly strong. I tried my best to resist, and so should you. Vocationally speaking, it's a terrible trap.

Third, the same argument about wealth applies to prestige. If you're aiming for something in life that will make people look up to you or admire you, you're aiming at the wrong thing. In the end, prestige counts for very little.

And besides, as our culture reminds us, prestige is a slippery thing. One day you have it, and the next day it's gone. The public tends to be fickle about its heroes, and the people we look up to today are often the people we despise tomorrow. The stories of certain politicians, pop-music icons, professional athletes, and corporate CEOs make that very clear.

> Discerning one's vocation relies on a process quite different from choosing a profession. A vocation must be heard or felt with passion. This passion — to write, to paint, to heal, to teach — must be confirmed first by oneself. Second, it needs to match one's gifts. And finally, it needs to be confirmed by a community of others or by a mentor. This final step helps preclude mistaking a personal compulsion with a genuine vocation.
>
> James Van Oosting, "Vocation Education," *America*

Fourth, sometimes people make career choices to hide from responsibility or to avoid being stretched. I've known people over the years who were extremely bright and capable, who had been given every opportunity to excel, but who, for various reasons, chose not to. They worked at jobs for which they were singularly overqualified. They knocked themselves out — or so it seemed — *not* to be noticed.

If you're doing what you're doing because it's safe, because it allows you to fly below life's radar, because you're motivated more by fear than anything else, then you've made a serious mistake with your life. Not only are your gifts going to waste, but you'll never know what you might have done with the gifts that God has given you.

I'm aware that some of the people who fall into this category actually have good reasons for living as they do. There are gifted people, for example, who suffer from social anxiety disorder, and they have chosen their jobs not because these positions fully utilize their gifts but because they provide a sense of safety. I know other gifted people who have taken extended leaves of absence to raise children or to care for elderly parents.

These are not the people I have in mind. I'm thinking of people here who, for other reasons entirely, have decided not to challenge themselves. These are often the people, in my experience, who wake up one day with a bad case of regret.

What about you? Are you playing it safe?

Fifth, there are individuals who actually do in life what they are wonderfully and naturally equipped to do, but — and this is enormously sad — they spend their lives with one eye fixed on other people. In other words, they've found their vocation, but they live with regret anyway — that they can't do it better than they do, that their accomplishments aren't recognized the way others' are, that their calling isn't as significant (let's say) as the calling that others have.

This issue is a recipe for disappointment and unhappiness and sometimes seething resentment in life. People who are following

God's call with their lives, who are using their gifts as they were meant to be used, need to keep their eyes focused on their own lives and their own calls.

Contentment comes when we stop measuring ourselves against standards set by others. Measuring success is often such a graceless exercise anyway. I realize that there are times and places in our lives when our performance needs to be objectively measured. As someone who works with a staff, I know all about job descriptions and performance reviews. What I have in mind here is very different. Vocation is ultimately about the relationship with the One who calls us. If vocational success can be measured at all, then maybe it can be measured best in terms of faithfulness to that relationship.

Sixth, low self-esteem may be the most common obstacle of all to finding God's call in our lives. There are people — and you may be one of them — who go through life continually underestimating their worth. Often feelings of low self-esteem come from our parents, but wherever they come from, they can poison our vocational lives. They undermine us in our attempts to be the people God has called us to be.

What I have learned from my faith is that I have been created in the image and likeness of God. Beyond that, God has equipped me to do something special, something needed, with my life. There can be no higher esteem, no higher stature within creation, than that.

So, please, don't underestimate your potential or your value. Consider, again, the story of Moses. He was in the desert in the first place, you remember, because he was a murderer and a fugitive. If God could take raw material like that and fashion him into one of Israel's most important leaders, then surely God can do something with you.

WHAT IS IT that you've been uniquely equipped to do with your life? Aren't you curious to find out?

QUESTIONS FOR REFLECTION AND DISCUSSION

1. Reread the story of Moses in the opening chapters of Exodus, especially the story of the call, which begins in chapter 3. What sort of process does Moses go through to get from his initial stance of resistance to his final stage of acceptance? What do you make of the questions he asks and the objections he raises? Have you ever struggled with God in a similar way?

2. In the discernment process, everyone takes a number of steps, deliberate or not, to figure out what God is saying. Where did you start (or where would you start today)? There are many gift inventories available, both in books and on Internet web sites. Have you ever done an assessment of your gifts? If you have, were there any surprises?

3. Have there been some "false starts" in your vocational life? Is there a way that you could reframe those experiences and begin to see them as important — even critical — learning experiences?

4. Review the six obstacles discussed in this chapter. Take them one by one and ask yourself — honestly — how am I doing with this? Do I let this obstacle get in the way of my calling?

✐ CHAPTER 5   *How Do I Achieve
Vocational Integrity?*

L ast summer I did something that was outside my comfort zone
— *way* outside it. I hadn't done anything like it since my college
days. And to be honest, even my college experience didn't prepare me
for this. For reasons I'm still not quite sure about, I agreed to take a
small part in a community theater production of *The Fantastiks.*

It's one of the longest-running musicals in Broadway history, and
nearly every community theater and high-school drama group has
produced it at least once. I played the part of Henry Albertson, a
washed-up actor who has an inflated sense of his own acting abilities.
Except for one — mercifully short — song at the end, I didn't have to
sing or dance. But I did have lines to learn.

Early on, soon after rehearsals started and word leaked out that
the pastor of the local Presbyterian church would be in an upcoming
show, a church member approached me one Sunday morning and
said, "Are you off book yet?"

I had no idea what he was talking about. I knew he'd been involved over the years in community theater, so I asked him what the
expression meant. He explained to me that all actors have to make
the transition from reading lines from a script to speaking them on

stage from memory. Getting "off book" means being able to set the script aside and, well, act.

When a production like *The Fantastiks* gets started, a few rehearsals at the beginning are devoted to something called "blocking." What happens is that actors walk around with scripts in hand and get a feel for the flow of the dialogue and where they're supposed to be on stage. Very soon, though, there's the expectation that actors will know both their places and their lines and won't have to refer to the script anymore.

But even that's not the final step. If you're good — in my case, a very big "if" — you'll move from simply reciting lines you've memorized to speaking those lines as though they come from deep within yourself.

I certainly don't claim to have reached that particular goal. But it became clear to me, over the course of the production, that the really gifted actors were able to memorize their lines and then internalize them, so that when they spoke, it was as though they became someone else entirely. Good actors, I imagine, live for those moments.

My acting career was mercifully short, and no other invitations to try out for other shows have been forthcoming. But I enjoyed this challenge, and I couldn't help thinking, during the course of the show, about the connection between acting and vocation. The question "Are you off book yet?" is really a question you could ask of anyone who's pursuing a vocation.

Any good friend, pastor, spouse, or mentor could probably ask that question of us from time to time.

Getting Off Book

As I see it, there are at least three distinct stages that we go through as we live vocationally — in other words, as we respond to the call of God in our lives.

The *first* is the sort of nervous but excited stage of having a script in hand and learning where we're supposed to be on stage. All of us go through it. Very few of us really like it, but it's nearly always a necessary first step. And it seems to me as though some people — not a lot, but some — never quite get beyond it.

If you move constantly in life from career to career, job to job, or life situation to life situation, you're always going to find yourself right there at the beginning, learning your lines, feeling your way. If you thrive on nervous excitement, that might be a good place to stay, but ultimately it's not very satisfying. Most us want to grow toward some measure of competence, a much higher comfort level, with what we're doing with our lives.

We get to the *second* stage of vocational life when we're finally able to put the script down and say our lines with a certain measure of confidence. It helps, of course, when the other people on stage know their lines. And if they say them the way we're expecting to hear them, we'll be okay — most of the time.

But, as I learned last summer, that's not really acting, and by extension I would say that's not really living the vocational life, either. If we've made it to this second stage of our life (and most people at midlife have made it this far), if we know our script well enough to repeat our lines on cue, we're doing well. But we haven't made it yet. There's at least one more stage involved.

And that *third* stage is living the part so completely that we don't even think about our lines anymore. We're not really worried about what other people on stage might say, either. Okay, we're somewhat concerned, but the point is, we've internalized our role. We've become who we were called to be. And so we even have the freedom to improvise. We don't improvise often, but the point is, we *could* do it. If the person next to us were to do something unexpected, we'd still know who we are and what's in character for us.

So, let me ask you again: Are you off book yet? Vocationally speaking, have you set aside the script? Or are you still reading your lines?

EARLY IN MY ministry, I was often surprised and a little taken aback to be called "Pastor" or "Reverend Brouwer." At the beginning I wore my title with a great deal of uncertainty and hesitation. I'm sure there are other newly ordained pastors who claim their titles more easily than I did, who look forward to their ordinations so that they can finally get started in their life's work. Some of my seminary classmates even started wearing clerical collars during their first year of study. But my pastoral identity grew slowly, so it always came as a shock to be addressed by my new title.

> Far from being of little or no spiritual account, then, human work is charged with religious significance — a significance which has been either wholly ignored or perverted by non-biblical attitudes toward work. . . . By working we affirm our uniquely human position as God's representatives on this earth, as cultivators and stewards of the good gifts of his creation, which are destined for the benefit of all.
>
> Lee Hardy,
> *The Fabric of This World*

I can't say exactly when things changed. I can tell you that it didn't happen my first week, month, or even year as a pastor. There was no particular day or hour when I suddenly felt comfortable with my role. But not long ago, while handling a crisis in the emergency room at the local hospital, I became aware — in a way I never had been before — that I knew who I was. And I was profoundly grateful to be that person.

A dear friend of mine, a man not much older than I am, had died very suddenly and unexpectedly. As soon as I heard the news, I drove over to the hospital to be with his wife. And I sat with her throughout the afternoon as, one by one, their four children came to the hospital and learned the painful truth about their dad.

It was one of the most difficult and exhausting days of my ministry, one I hope never to repeat, but there was one gratifying aspect of it: I knew what to do. I knew how to respond. As painful as it was, I felt utterly at ease in my role. I was glad, in a way, that I could be present for the family of my friend. No matter what happened that afternoon, I believed that I would be up to the challenge. I wasn't reciting lines anymore. I was a pastor, and without having to think about it, I did my job as well as I was able to do it. I knew that day that I was off book.

The Problem with Work

Many people I know have ambivalent feelings about their work. They love their lives; it's their jobs they could do without. It's hard for them to believe that work is what they were meant to do for the rest of their lives. And so, for many of them, the whole aim of life seems to be to work just hard enough, just long enough, so that they don't have to work anymore.

I can't be the only person who listens with fascination to lottery winners in the first hours after they win their prizes. Quite often, these brand-new multimillionaires will say on-camera that their immediate plan is to walk into the boss's office the very next morning and quit. Some say that they're going to tell him what he can do with his job.

Occasionally a winner will say that she's going to work for as long as she possibly can, but the majority of winners, according to lottery officials, don't continue to work, even when they at first plan to stay at their jobs. Apparently, after they achieve financial security, a job no longer seems to make sense.

I read recently that a large percentage of lottery winners file for bankruptcy in the first five years after they win, which leads me to think that they have, among other problems, a deeply flawed understanding of the meaning and purpose of life. Having a job doesn't automatically give life meaning and purpose, but giving up a job can easily rob life of these things.

The ambiguity of work actually has quite a long history. Even the book of Genesis has been interpreted by some to mean that work itself is cursed. Before the Fall, life was good and pleasant, but after the Fall, some believe, Adam and Eve had to labor and sweat, as though work itself became the punishment for their sin.

That understanding of those early chapters of the Bible — work as punishment — is widespread, but I believe it's wrong.

According to Genesis, when God first created human beings, they were given tasks and responsibilities. Life was good, but it wasn't without work. The work itself was good and pleasant, even life-giving. God blessed them by giving them work to do. So, in the beginning human beings found meaning and purpose *in their work*. After the Fall, however, work became less pleasant and often extremely difficult. As a result of the broken relationship, work became separated from meaning and purpose.

THE ANCIENT GREEKS weren't just ambivalent toward work; they detested it. They thought work was suitable for slaves, but they thought most people should avoid work and devote themselves entirely to leisure. Plato didn't like work, but he didn't have much use for leisure, either. He once wrote that leisure was for grazing animals who spend their lives "feeding, fattening, and fornicating." So Plato urged the people of Athens to devote themselves to the life of the mind, to ideas and contemplation, which to his way of thinking wasn't quite the same thing as leisure.

> In following your proper calling, no work will be so mean and sordid as not to have splendor and value in the eye of God.
>
> John Calvin, *Institutes*

It wasn't until the Reformation — the sixteenth century — that people like Martin Luther and John Calvin, two towering figures in Protestant history, said unequivocally that work was good. In fact, they said, work was the way we honored God with our lives. But God wasn't the only one who benefited. Luther and Calvin argued that human beings found meaning and worth in their work, no matter how menial it might be. Work gave human beings a certain stature, a certain dignity within creation.

In recent years, a number of important Christian thinkers have argued that, while work may once have had meaning and value, it no longer does. Jacques Ellul, a French scholar who writes about political and social philosophy from a faith perspective, is one such example. According to Ellul, technology and modern life in general have rendered most work meaningless. It doesn't make sense, he and others say, to think of most work these days in terms of vocation.

As you read Ellul's writings, you might begin to think that your current work is meaningless. Or you may remember a job along the way that seemed to serve no purpose whatsoever. The truth is, most of us have had jobs at one time or another that seemed pointless, that didn't seem to serve God or anyone else.

And yet, as important as these critiques are, I still believe that vocation is an idea that has merit, an idea that's critically important for people today. Not every job we hold will, in itself, be a way of loving God and neighbor, but the category of vocation asks us to think in significantly broader terms. Vocation, as I've tried to argue here, is more than what we do; to a surprising degree, our vocation is who we are. When we live our lives "off book," we become the person we were created and called to be.

MOST PEOPLE of faith today, whether they realize it or not, are products of the Reformation — or at least the way of thinking about work that took hold during the Reformation. We tend to place a high value on work, we hold those who work hard in high regard, and we expect our children to be hard workers.

Over the years I've lived in communities where there is an undeniably strong work ethic. My neighbors seldom, if ever, take long vacations or speak much about leisure time. Retired people I know do sometimes take long vacations, if they have the resources, but not working people, not the people in my neighborhoods, even when they have the resources to do so. The neighbors I have known over the years are much more likely to talk about how busy they are, how many demands there are on their time, how difficult it is for them to get away.

Interestingly, we tend to admire and look up to those who work long hours. One of my former neighbors was a merger and acquisitions attorney for a downtown Chicago law firm. He would leave his house well before six each morning to catch an early train to his office. I would wave good-bye when I went out to get the morning newspaper. He seldom returned home before seven in the evening. It wasn't unusual for him to work Saturdays and Sundays as well. He seldom took a day off.

Most of us in the neighborhood thought highly of him. I confess that I did too. He was an extraordinarily hard worker, after all, and a model of industry and productivity. And he provided exceptionally well for his family.

When I was growing up, my parents were concerned that I "make something of myself." Somehow I knew that to "make something of myself" I couldn't take a casual approach to life. The phrase implied ambition and a desire to reach as far as my gifts would take me. Many others must have heard similar words from their parents. And the result is that for most of my life I've lived in communities where nearly all of my neighbors have worked extremely hard to make something of themselves.

What about you? Are you working hard to "make something of yourself"? Here's my guess: A strong work ethic may well be a trait to admire in ourselves and other people, but this ethic by itself won't lead to a sense of meaning and purpose in life.

If you're going to work hard, if you're going to give your life to something, let it be to something that's worthy of your time and your gifts. Let it be to something that serves God and neighbor.

SOME PEOPLE look at my work, the life of parish ministry, and they say, "No wonder you like what you do. No wonder you're willing to work long days and answer the phone at all hours. You're making a difference in the lives of people. My own work will soon be forgotten. No one really cares much what I do. But yours is different."

At a reception for new church members not long ago, I spoke with a man who works for a major corporation in the area of information technology — clearly very different from parish ministry. When I asked him to explain more fully what he did, he said, without expression, "One day I dig a hole, and the next day I fill it back up again. At least that's the way it feels."

I didn't know what to say. I think I said, "I'm sorry." And I was — for him and for everyone who is in a similar position.

Could you hear yourself saying something like that? If you won a big lottery jackpot today, what would you do? Many people have fantasized about it, even if they've never purchased a ticket. Would you continue to work? If so, why?

Finding Integrity in Our Work

One way to find meaning in our work is to think of it as vocation. But as important as I think vocation is, I'm aware that merely thinking of what we do as our calling may not be enough, may not change our attitudes toward it.

If you don't like your work, or you don't like your place in life right now, putting a thin veneer of vocation over the top of it won't change a thing. I wish finding integrity in your work could be that easy. You may disguise the truth for a while, but sooner or later you'll discover what you've done. You can't fake a call.

In the last few years I've had more breakfasts and lunches with people who feel stuck in their lives than you can possibly imagine. I've lost count of the number. So many of us wish we could be doing something different with our lives. So many of us feel called to do something more.

Occasionally I'll challenge these people to make a change, to take the risk of finding something new, but often I'll find myself simply agreeing that their work — whatever it is — doesn't seem to have a lot of meaning and that there isn't an obvious way out. Very often, in fact, I'll say that for the sake of the kids, or the marriage, or the elderly parents, or the college tuition payments, or whatever it is, these people ought to stay put. In other words, they should just keep doing what they've been doing, even though their work isn't very satisfying and by itself can hardly be called their vocation.

> Now there are varieties of gifts, but the same Spirit; and there are varieties of services, but the same Lord; and there are varieties of activities, but it is the same God who activates all of them in everyone. To each is given the manifestation of the Spirit for the common good.
>
> 1 Corinthians 12:4-7, NRSV

But that doesn't seem like enough, does it? There must be more that can be said. In my reading about vocation I've discovered a few ways that people of faith use to stay in difficult jobs or difficult life situations — without losing their integrity or their minds.

Here are three ideas. They may not all work for you, but one of them may be just enough to keep you going.

First, if you feel stuck, but for a variety of reasons need to stay where you are, find other ways to serve, to give generously of yourself. After all, as I've argued here, the basic truth of vocational life is to "love God and love your neighbor as yourself." Sometimes, by doing our jobs differently, by seeing the people around us differently, by seeing our workplace as a place in which to do ministry, we can transform a "stuck" situation into something more.

Frankly, I hope people of faith do this anyway. Wherever you are during the week, you can serve the people around you, but if you're in a tough situation, it's possible that you need to hear this reminder or encouragement. Try seeing your coworkers as people like you who were created in the image and likeness of God, people with real needs and sometimes difficult concerns. You might be surprised to learn that your vocation, your true vocation, is to be there for them.

But there are still other ways to serve. Some people who don't like their jobs find other settings in their lives in which to use their gifts. The churches I've served are the grateful recipients of numerous hours of work each week, often given by people who can't offer their finest gifts in their work situations.

One former church member who became a dear friend sells insurance. He seems to be good at what he does, and he's certainly successful as popular culture defines success. But I've noticed that his passion isn't insurance; it's scouting. He earned his Eagle Scout award as a teenager and continues to be active in scouting today. He believes strongly in scouting ideals and still lives by them. Whenever I think of a Boy Scout, I will always think of him.

A few years ago I asked him to speak in worship. The assigned topic was stewardship, and previous speakers had talked about giving their talents or their treasure. The gift he felt most able to give, he said, was time. And he then spoke movingly about feeling called to work with young men, including his two sons, and to teach them some of the things that had been and remain so important in his own life. For him, scouting is as powerful a call as any I've ever known.

To repeat the point: For many of us, the work we do is not, nor will it ever be, our vocation. When it's necessary for us to continue working at jobs that are not our vocations, we can nevertheless find ways to live and work with integrity. Sometimes our vocation will be alongside, or in addition to, our work.

Second, find balance in your life. I'll have more to say about this in another chapter, so at this point I'll simply state that one way to survive a tough work situation or a tough life situation is to be intentional about finding spiritual and emotional renewal, to continue to replenish our inner resources. I'm not talking about taking a vacation, though that could be part of it. I'm really talking about something more. I'm talking, I suppose, about an active, satisfying spiritual life.

I read an article once about the way that kids, primarily teenagers, spend their time. More and more kids today participate in sports, and studies show that that's good. But only to a point. Kids who play sports do better in school, have greater self-esteem, and experiment less with drugs, alcohol, and sex. After a certain point, though, there appear to be diminishing returns. Too much of any extracurricular activity, researchers found, can itself be a problem.

Sean Covey, son of time-management guru Stephen Covey, says that our lives have four critical areas — physical, mental, social, and spiritual. "It's like four wheels on a car," Covey says. "If one tire is low, all four will wear unevenly."

I like that image. To live our lives fully and with integrity, we're going to need balance among all key areas of our lives. Parents need to provide that for their children, and we need to provide that for ourselves. What are you doing to maintain balance in your life?

Third, try a novel way to approach a "stuck" job: do it well, as well as it can be done. Do it better than you ever expected yourself to do it. Work for excellence (which is not quite the same thing as perfectionism), strive for truth (but watch out for the self-righteousness that often goes with it), and be diligent as well as persistent (while trying very hard not to be fanatical).

Not long ago, during a low period of my ministry, when I wasn't feeling particularly energized in my work and wasn't seeing many results, I took this little bit of advice to heart. I started to give my work everything I had. Instead of slowing down and giving in to the malaise I was feeling, I sped up. I started new programs. I looked for new ideas to pursue. And guess what? It helped. The problems didn't go away, and I didn't expect them to, but other things began to seem more important than the problems I had been encountering. And the unexpected bonus was that my energy and investment of time was good for the morale of those around me. Others began to work harder too.

Before I ran my first Chicago marathon in 1999, I received a similar bit of advice from a more experienced runner. He told me that when I hit the wall at the eighteen- or twenty-mile mark, when I started to feel as though I had nothing more to draw on — something that nearly all marathoners experience for physiological reasons that I don't pretend to understand — I should try speeding up just a bit. Not a lot, he said, but pick up the pace. Don't give in to the temptation to slow down or stop. Do something unexpected. Work harder.

At the time I didn't think much of that advice. To tell you the truth, it sounded odd. But there I was on race day, at the eighteen- or twenty-mile mark, with Comiskey Park (now U.S. Cellular Field) in sight, and I was ready to call it quits. I was sore and tired. I was chafing in places I didn't know I could chafe. I had nothing left to give. So I did the unexpected thing. I picked up the pace — just slightly. Maybe no one out there noticed but me, but I was aware of what I had done.

Where in your life do you need to pick up the pace?

QUESTIONS FOR REFLECTION AND DISCUSSION

1. Can you think of a time in your life when you finally felt "off book," as though you were pursuing your vocation fully and completely, without the need for a script?

2. Jacques Ellul and other thinkers have argued that work itself has lost much of its meaning because of technology and other modern advances. Do you feel that way about the work you do? Do you sense that your work doesn't make much of a difference to anyone? If so, what are some things you could do, either on the job or in addition to it, that would give your life a renewed sense of meaning and purpose? Is it time to think of your vocation as something larger than what you do?

3. One way to find balance in life is to cultivate your spiritual life. Some people, when they hear that, think of daily Bible reading, which they've tried in the past but haven't been able to sustain. What would a deeper spiritual life look like for you? More than simply activities — like Bible reading, let's say — what would you need to do in order to have a better, more satisfying spiritual life?

CHAPTER 6

How Do I Live with Joy in the Face of Disappointment?

Many of us took piano lessons when we were growing up, but not all of us became Billy Joel. Many of us played high-school sports, but not all of us became Jackie Joyner-Kersee. Many of us studied hard in school, but not all of us became rocket scientists.

The truth is, we weren't able to become everything we ever dreamed of being. Dealing with limitations and discovering that not every path in life is open to us must be a near-universal experience. Along the way, some of us learned to accept our limitations and move on more gracefully and with more good humor than others. But most of us eventually acknowledge what we can't do and focus instead on what we can do.

In my experience, though, there's actually more to the story than that. I've noticed that many of us struggle not simply with limitations, but with something much deeper and more difficult. What we struggle with, I think, is disappointment, loss, and failure *within our vocations.* When we think we've actually found something in life that we can do well, that we've been called to do, and then realize that the path ahead is closed to us or that we're no longer needed or that we didn't make the cut, that's when the disappointment or pain is most acute.

The spiritual question, as I see it, is this: How do you live your life with faith, hope, and joy when doors close in your face? Some people I know — God bless them — live their lives with the sincere belief that when one door closes, another always opens. But is that really so?

I wish it were, but I'm not so sure. It hasn't always been true in my experience.

So I wonder: What does a person of faith say in the face of life's inevitable limitations and disappointments? What is there to say when life doesn't unfold as we expected, as we were convinced it would?

Dreams and Vocations

I think it's critically important to distinguish between dreams and vocations. They aren't always the same.

Recently a friend who lives and works in New York City sent me an e-mail. He's the pastor of a church there, and he told me that he had visited my church's web site and listened to one of my sermons on vocation. And, like a good colleague, he wanted to quibble with a point I had made.

My friend told me about one of his church members who is a waitress. According to my friend, if you ask her what she does, she will say, "I'm an actress. I may wait tables, but I'm really an actress waiting to be discovered." My friend told me that there are, in fact, several people just like her in his congregation — artists, musicians, dancers, as well as actors, many of whom are working at entry-level, minimum-wage jobs while they wait, not always in good humor, for their big breaks.

Here's the question my friend posed to me. "Are we doing these people a disservice?" he asked. "They've been encouraged from a young age, by their parents, by their teachers, and by their church, to do something special, something unique, with their lives. They've all been told to pursue their dreams and not to let go of them. So, here they are — well into their thirties and forties, in some cases — and most of them are never going to get the big break they've been hoping for. How do we talk to them about vocation when there's such a huge disconnect between what they do and what they dream about doing with their lives?"

I was never aware of any waitresses in the churches I've served who were hoping to land big-time acting jobs. The communities in which those churches were located wouldn't have been great places to live if you were hoping to be discovered. But, like my friend, I do know a few people who are doing one thing with their lives while hoping to do something completely different. They seem intent on pursuing a dream that, to most people, looks out of reach for them.

My pastor's heart wants to encourage them. I want more than anything for these people to realize their dreams. But there's a part of me that wants to say, "Isn't it time for you to let go of that particular dream? Isn't it time to recognize the difference between a dream and a vocation? What you're pursuing may have seemed like your vocation at one point in your life, and maybe you even have some gifts for it. But what you're pursuing is more of a dream than a vocation. For your own sake, move on with your life."

> Each of us is given a nature by God. To have a nature is to have both limits and potentials. We can learn as much about God-given nature by running into our limits as by experiencing our potentials. . . . The truth is that I cannot be anything I want to be or do anything I want to do. The truth is that my created nature, my God-given nature makes me like an organism in an ecosystem: I thrive in some roles and relationships within that system, but in others I wither and die.
>
> Parker Palmer, "On Minding Our Calls," *Weavings*

SOMETIMES THE DREAMS people have for their lives aren't work- or career-related.

I know people — women and men — who want to be married. They want more than anything to be in the sort of relationship in which they would be able to give and receive love. But, in spite of their deepest longings, marriage never seems to happen for them.

I've also known couples who want to be parents, who want more than anything to conceive a child, who have spent thousands of dollars to no avail on a variety of fertility treatments. To them it's a crushing disappointment to reach midlife and not be able to start a family.

I've known still other people who have kind and generous hearts. They want more than anything to be in the sort of careers that would allow them to listen and care and love. They're convinced that would be their true calling. But instead they find themselves, let's say, in a corporate setting where listening and caring and loving are all well and good, but not the basis for the bonuses at the end of the year. So they languish. They feel frustrated or, worse, they feel unappreciated, as though their special gifts are going to waste.

What do we say to these people? What have *you* said as you've listened to people like this?

I'll be honest. My own responses haven't always been good ones. It's hard for me to listen when I think I know what another person should do. And so, occasionally, sorry to say, I've learned what not to say by saying the wrong thing.

To a single person who wants very much to be married, for example, I now know that "Be the best single person you can be" is not such a helpful response. In certain situations, I now realize, it can sound uncaring and patronizing. As with most vocational questions and struggles, the best response any of us can make is simply to be a caring presence.

Walking alongside those who struggle, often without saying anything at all, can be a far more helpful response than offering unwanted and possibly misguided advice.

IN THESE SITUATIONS, the pastoral response is to be a non-anxious presence. The response of a good friend or family member is to listen, to be emotionally available. But how are we supposed to understand the *dynamics* of these situations?

One way, I believe, is to distinguish between dreams and vocations, which is admittedly a difficult distinction to make. After all, dreams and vocations often overlap each other. It's often difficult to know where one ends and the other begins. Distinguishing between dreams and vocations, I would say, is ultimately a part of the discernment process I described in an earlier chapter.

My childhood desire to be a professional baseball player now seems more like a dream than anything else, totally unrelated to what I would describe as my vocation today. I was in high school when I realized that, no matter how much I loved the game, I wasn't going anywhere as a player. No matter how much of myself I gave to the game, I was never going to be more than mediocre. Today I can say I'm glad I did. Though it was somewhat painful, I let go of that particular dream and moved on with my life.

Other dreams can't so obviously be separated from vocation. My suspicion is that the waitress in my friend's church is, at this point in her life, pursuing a dream and not a vocation. I suspect, though I don't know this for sure, that she's holding onto her dream for some unhealthy reasons. As it is, she's having a very difficult time living vocationally, being the person God has called her to be.

Maybe (a good friend or family member would have to approach this subject with a great deal of discretion and sensitivity) her situation is a clue that God is actually calling her in a different direction, which leads me to another way of thinking about this issue.

When One Door Closes . . .

People who have listened to me preach over the years know that I dislike certain bromides or adages that Christian people like to pass off as biblical truths. One of my least favorite is "God doesn't give us any more than we can handle."

That grates on me. I think I know why people use it, but theologically I don't think it stands up. The expression, taken at face value, seems to imply that God deals out difficult circumstances, but is compassionate or loving enough to stop short of our breaking points.

The more the expression is repeated, the more people begin to think that there might be some truth to it. Some people, I've noticed, think it might be in the Bible. The Old Testament? Proverbs, maybe? It's got to be there somewhere, they say.

Here's another one I like even less: "When one door closes, another always opens."

I know I sound like a curmudgeon here, but I can't help it. I just can't stand that expression. On the other hand, I usually like the people who use it. I like the attitude it represents. We're all drawn to optimists, aren't we? They're the people who always seem to land on their feet after a tough experience. So my problem isn't with the people who repeat those words and live their lives with a glass-half-full kind of outlook on life. My problem is with the words themselves.

Is it true that another door always opens when one closes, when we experience a crushing disappointment in our lives?

PARKER PALMER, whose writing about vocation I mentioned in my opening chapter, has taken this old saying and enlarged on it. As he puts it, "When one door closes, the whole world opens up."

When I first read those words, my inclination was to dismiss this new expression as quickly as its first cousin. But then, after a minute or two, I had to agree that maybe there was something to it after all.

Sometimes disappointment in life, a closed door, is precisely the occasion that it takes for us to discover our true calling in life. Sometimes a closed door gives us a kind of clarity about our lives that we've never had before. Sometimes a bump on the head is more than that — sometimes it has a way of knocking some sense into us. I've had a few bumps like that along the way. I'm guessing you have too.

And yet, I must say, Palmer's expression still troubles me. I wonder if it's really sound theology. Like its first cousin, it seems to imply that something good will always happen soon after something bad. But is that true? Is that a perspective that's grounded anywhere in the Bible? The answer, I have to say, is no.

Sometimes when a door closes in our lives, about three others will close at exactly the same time. I wish it weren't so, but my experience tells me it is. When it rains, it pours. (Now there's an expression that may have some merit.) Or sometimes a door will close in our lives, and another door won't open for a long, long time.

One time I heard a comedian — a *Christian* comedian — say, "When one door closes, a trap door opens up." He got a big laugh because, well, sometimes it's true.

There is absolutely no promise anywhere in the Christian faith that everything in our lives will work out to our advantage — at least not right away. The Apostle Paul at one point does say that "everything works together for good for those who love God and are called according to his purpose." But I usually point out in Bible-study settings that Paul might have been thinking there about the distant future, about the life after this one.

So, okay, *eventually* things will work out for our good, but today? Not guaranteed. Tomorrow? It would be nice, wouldn't it? But we don't know. Next year? No one knows. Someday.

So what does the Christian faith have to say about closed doors? Quite a lot, to be honest about it. The Bible contains story after story about people of faith who face difficult situations and disappointments in their lives. My faith tells me that we can't do or be everything in life that we dream of doing or being. We can do some things, but not every single thing. Not every door will open to us, no matter how long we wait.

IF ALL OF THAT sounds just a bit discouraging, let me offer some good news: God doesn't send evil our way. This is a truth that ought to be mentioned much more often than it is. God isn't the author of evil, and God doesn't send evil into our lives. The disappointments, failures, and closed doors we experience are not of God. They aren't.

God can, however, make something good come out of them. God can use them, for example, to steer us in a new direction. But — and this is critically important to see — God doesn't hurl tough times our way to see what kind of stuff we're made of.

> If I develop one gift, it means that other gifts will not be used. Doors will close on a million lovely possibilities. I will become a painter or a doctor only if denial becomes a part of my picture of reality. Commitment at the point of my gifts means that I must give up being a straddler. Somewhere in the depths of me I know this. . . . My commitment will give me an identity. When asked who I am, I will be reminded that the answer lies in the exercise of my gifts.
>
> Elizabeth O'Connor, *The Eighth Day of Creation: Gifts and Creativity*

What kind of God would that be? Would you create a major disappointment for one of your children just to see what kind of response you'd get? No? Then why do Christian people insist that God creates disappointments — or closes doors? That doesn't seem consistent to me with the God I know about from reading the Bible. I know that there are references in the Bible to wilderness periods of life and to times of testing, but people of faith have never believed that God deliberately sends evil into our lives.

I'm reminded here of a very moving sermon by William Sloane Coffin, the former chaplain at Yale University and later the preacher at Riverside Church in New York City. "Alex's Death" is probably the sermon for which he'll always be remembered. It's one of the most helpful and powerful pieces ever written or preached about death, grief, and the will of God. Written just days after the tragic death of his son, Coffin hammers home this one truth: God didn't cause his son's death:

> It was not the will of God that Alex die. . . . When the waves closed over the sinking car, God's heart was the first of all our hearts to break.

Coffin probably needed to hear that message as much as anyone who was in worship that day. The good news in the face of life's disappointments and tragedies is not that "God doesn't give us any more than we can handle." It's that God is right there with us, always faithful.

MY OWN JOURNEY into the Presbyterian Church occurred at a time of major disappointment, one of the biggest of my life. I didn't grow up Presbyterian and didn't set out to become a Presbyterian. In fact, I had no desire to become one, and I couldn't imagine at the time how life as a Presbyterian might be.

Through a troubling series of circumstances — primarily my choice of seminary, which seemed like the right choice for me at the time — I was faced at an early point in my preparation for ministry with leaving the denomination of my childhood and finding a new church home. It doesn't sound like all that much now, not even to me, but at the time I was as discouraged and dejected as I have ever been. What happened came as a crushing blow. I lost weight, I couldn't sleep, and though it was never diagnosed, I'm fairly certain now that I sank into a moderate depression, one that lasted for several months.

Did God do that to me? I have never for one moment entertained the possibility. That's not the God I know. But I do know that God took the situation, difficult as it was for me, and somehow got my attention through it. I believe now that God made something good, even life-giving, happen as a result of something truly, unspeakably painful. A door closed in my life, and — eventually, though not right away — another opened.

Did the whole world open up? In a way, yes. A world I had never considered suddenly became possible. When I became a Presbyterian, as a matter of fact, I experienced a taste of God's grace. I will never forget the welcome and embrace I received.

So, doors close. They close all the time, and I believe that those are occasions in our lives that we need to pay attention to. At a spiritual level, we need to be alert because, more than likely, God is at work in those moments.

Seize Life!

One of the genres of biblical literature that I discovered relatively late in my faith journey is wisdom literature. Found primarily in the Old Testament, wisdom books include Proverbs, Ecclesiastes, and Job. Scholars believe that some psalms and possibly a few chapters from other books belong to the genre as well.

Writers of wisdom literature took a very realistic view of life. They didn't waste time on false hope or wishful thinking. When they could, they tended to take life in stride, the good along with the bad. The person who wrote Ecclesiastes sounds old and weary — *world* weary — as though he's seen all there is to see. But he's not without hope. And he's not without joy.

On a tired, wrinkled face you can still see a little smile and maybe a twinkle in his eyes.

And this is what he says: Seize life. Carpe diem. Don't skimp on the good things. Take pleasure in your lives because, after all, life is a gift. Never forget that. *Life is a gift.* So make the most of every single day. If you spend all of your time thinking about what a raw deal you got or how someone betrayed you or why things aren't turning out as you had hoped, you'll miss the best part of your life.

The verse I particularly like is Ecclesiastes 9:10. In the version of Scripture called The Message, it reads like this: "Whatever turns up, grab it and do it. And heartily!" The New Revised Standard Version puts it this way: "Whatever your hand finds to do, do [it] with [all] your might." If the author of Ecclesiastes were writing today, he might have used the expression "Grip it and rip it!" Grab hold of life and give it all you've got.

I know there are people who live with terrible disappointments. All I can say to them — all I can say to you — is this: Our faith calls us to

> Seize life! Eat bread with gusto.
> Drink wine with a robust heart.
> Oh yes — God takes pleasure in your pleasure!
> Dress festively every morning.
> Don't skimp on colors and scarves.
> Relish life with the spouse you love
> Each and every day of your precious life.
> Each day Is God's gift. It's all you get in exchange
> For the hard work of staying alive.
> Make the most of each one!
> Whatever turns up, grab it and do it. And heartily!
>
> Ecclesiastes 9:7-10, The Message

find a way to live, to celebrate the gift of life. So when a ray of hope, faint or otherwise, comes your way, camp under it, enjoy it, and linger there for as long as you can. If ten things happen to you today, and nine of them are sad, then cling with all your might to the one good thing. Because that one good thing will be God's gift to you.

Seize life!

QUESTIONS FOR REFLECTION AND DISCUSSION

1. Where have doors closed in your life? Go back in your memory and write them down. Now think about what was helpful and what wasn't as you worked your way through these situations. What enabled you to get through? What obstacles were in your way? What moments of grace and humor did you experience?

2. Is there a closed door in your life right now? How are you dealing with it?

Keeping in mind Parker Palmer's words about the "whole world" opening up, are you able to see this closed door as something different, as a time of unprecedented opportunity? Is it possible that God is using this disappointment to offer you something new and unexpected?

3. I end this chapter with a reference to the wisdom literature of the Old Testament. Some wisdom literature is very positive and optimistic; some, like Job, is not. The book of Ecclesiastes is hard to label exactly, but it does have a point of view. Read 9:7-10 — which appear in a sidebar above — and reflect on the vocational message of those verses. How do they apply to your life?

 **CHAPTER 7** *How Do I Pursue My Vocation beyond My Career?*

John Elway was the winningest quarterback in NFL history. In 1999 he did something that few other professional athletes have been able to do. After a sixteen-year career, he walked away from the game he loved, and, remarkably enough, he stayed away. He quit, most agree, at the top of his game.

Along the way, Elway apparently made all the money he would ever need to live comfortably, so at the end of the 1999 season, after finally taking his team, the Denver Broncos, to the Super Bowl, he simply said good-bye to the game he had been involved with, in one way or another, his entire life.

Sadly, his life since retirement hasn't been filled with triumph and personal accomplishment. Just the opposite, in fact. Within two years of his retirement, Elway's father, his biggest fan and promoter since childhood, died suddenly of a heart attack. Most of his business ventures flopped, including one highly publicized online sporting goods business, in which Michael Jordan and Wayne Gretzky were partners. His wife, Janet, the person to whom he had been married for eighteen years, left him and took their four children with her. And then, shortly after that, Elway's twin sister died of lung cancer.

To say that John Elway's life after football has been difficult would be an understatement. He was interviewed in the months after his sister's death, and he said something to the reporter that caught my attention. Without a sense of purpose and direction, without a goal in life, he admitted, his retirement had been a disaster.

He was only forty-four when he made that statement, so he still has time to get his life back on track. But I think there's something terribly urgent to be learned from the life of this sports legend: Not only is it vitally important to have a sense of meaning and purpose in your work life. It's every bit as important to have a sense of meaning and purpose in retirement.

I MADE A FRIEND soon after I moved to the Chicago area. He seemed to be successful in just about everything he did. Money always seemed to flow in his general direction. And I must say, he was fun to be around. The party always seemed to start when he showed up.

One time, when I asked him about his personal goals, he told me that his plan in life was to bank about fifteen million (which seemed within easy reach in the late 1990s, when the stock market set new upside records every day), retire at age fifty, and then move to a sailboat on Catalina Island, just off the coast of southern California.

> My whole life I had something to chase. For sixteen years winning the Super Bowl was my carrot. Everything revolved around that. All of a sudden there's no carrot anymore, and you start wondering what you're going to do with your life. You play golf or you try business stuff, but it's not even close. You end up spinning yourself like a tornado. And here was Janet, who sacrificed all those years, thinking she was finally going to get me to herself.
>
> John Elway, retired
> NFL quarterback

"And then what?" I asked.

"Sail," he said. "Live. Enjoy life."

Looking back, I think I was too startled to have much of a reaction. I had never known a person quite like this. I had never heard anyone lay out such an ambitious plan. Only later, much later, did it occur to me that something important was missing from this plan. And today what I would say is that my friend's plan sounds empty and shallow and, like John's Elway's life, maybe, headed for disaster.

What the Bible Says

I think it's important to come clean at the beginning of this chapter and admit that the Bible says almost nothing about retirement. Not directly, anyway. I doubt that there's even a Hebrew word for retirement. It just wasn't something that the ancients thought much about. It hasn't been until the last hundred years or so, with rising life expectancies and the affluence of the industrialized world, that retirement has even been within the reach of most people.

The Bible may not say much about retirement, but it has a great deal to say about life in general — what makes for a good and full life, and of course what leads to disappointment and occasionally to disaster in life. The Bible is filled with examples of both, especially the latter. And what the Bible seems to say, over and over again, in both Old and New Testaments, is that a good and full life, a life filled with meaning and purpose, is ordinarily a life lived in faithfulness, in service — to God and other people.

So, would you like to know what the Bible and Christian faith have to say about living a life full of meaning and purpose? I'll tell you: Give yourself away. That's it. If you do that, you'll have all the meaning and purpose you can handle. On the other hand, as soon as you make yourself the center and chief goal of your life, you'll be in trouble. Maybe not right away, but soon enough.

I'll tell you something else the Bible says. The Bible is clear about the need for balance, for regular intervals of rest and recovery. The creation story in Genesis is a reminder that balance has been woven into the very fabric of the created order. We were created for work, yes, but that work must also be balanced with rest and play. God went so far as to command the people of Israel, in the giving of the Ten Commandments, to take time off from work. For one day each and every week, God said, let it go, all of it. Don't work. In fact, give your entire household a day off each week.

I think the idea of retirement, though it was unknown in the world that produced the Bible, is consistent with what we believe about the created order. People who work their entire lives at sometimes-difficult jobs may, if they are able to, let them go and walk away. Many people who retire, it seems to me, are entitled to a time of rest in their lives, a time to step back and enjoy the work they have accomplished.

> And on the seventh day God finished the work that he had done, and he rested on the seventh day from all the work that he had done. So God blessed the seventh day and hallowed it, because on it God rested from all the work that he had done in creation.
>
> Genesis 2:2-3, NRSV

The New Testament assumes much of what the Old Testament teaches and adds to it. Jesus himself seems to have internalized Old Testament teachings. The Gospels point out how Jesus, from the beginning of his ministry, even when he seemed to be needed the most, made balance a part of his life and escaped for brief periods of rest and spiritual replenishment. He engaged people intensely for a time, but then he managed to withdraw. He thoroughly enjoyed the company of friends and family, and he gave himself generously to the crowds who followed him. But he also enjoyed time alone.

It's a pattern that I think we need to pay attention to. The problem is, few people seem to know how to do it.

FINDING BALANCE seems out of reach for most of the people I know. Some people deceive themselves into thinking that juggling a large number of activities, including church, is the same as leading a balanced life. I'm afraid it isn't. Successfully juggling a busy schedule still means being busy. The problem for most of us, I'm convinced, is that we simply don't know how to say no. We don't know how to slow down and take on fewer responsibilities.

Sorry to say, the church sends lots of mixed signals on this subject. On the one hand, we encourage our people to find time for the primary relationships in life, including our relationship with God. On the other hand, we depend on church members to make our programs and ministries work. Unfortunately, being busy at church is not the same thing as having a vibrant spiritual life. I'm ashamed to say that I've never told anyone that serving a term on the Buildings and Grounds Committee is not the same thing as spending more time with God.

At the church I served in Wheaton, we did try something new. We decided to take the season of Advent seriously. Advent is a time to be quiet, to watch for God's work in the work of the world, to cultivate the discipline of waiting with expectation. So we agreed that church members should be at home with their families and not at church attending meetings. We specifically told all committees not to hold meetings unless they were absolutely necessary.

Not surprisingly, this decision was received enthusiastically. After all, who wouldn't want another free night or two during the holidays? Still, the experiment wasn't an unqualified success. In our review after the season was over, church members told us that they simply found other things to do — attending parties and fulfilling seasonal obligations.

But I was glad to discover that the very next year church members asked for the same kind of Advent observance. We had at least planted the idea that there was another way to get ready for Christmas. I suspect that something similar will have to happen in the rest of our lives. Years of bad habits will take time to undo. What's important, though, is to get started, to make the effort, to cultivate balance as a way of life.

Careers and Vocations

Vocation, as we've seen, has more to do with who we are than with what we happen to do. Our careers seldom are the same thing as our vocations. That's a critically important distinction to keep in mind as we think about leisure and even retirement. For many if not most people, a career is the job we do to provide for our families, but it's not necessarily who we are or what we're called to be.

I'm a Presbyterian pastor. I earn my living by providing a number of services to the congregations I serve. Some of those services are closely related to my call, and some are not. I believe that my primary calling in life is to be a communicator and teacher of the Christian faith. After a long, long process of discernment, that's how I would describe my vocation.

I think I have gifts for preaching, teaching, and writing. I also believe I'm a compassionate person and am reasonably effective as a leader. So I feel called to walk with people during the difficult times of their lives. And I've been able to manage large staffs, budgets, and properties. But I'm still certain of my primary vocation. I'm most effective as a preacher, teacher, and writer — far less so as a caregiver and manager.

Putting all of my gifts together has made me, over the years, an effective pastor. But being a pastor is not, strictly speaking, my calling; it's my career. In one way or another I plan to continue to pursue my calling throughout my life. At some point, if health and financial resources permit, I would love to retire from parish ministry and pursue my vocation full-time.

In other words — and this is a critical point — in retirement we don't stop being the people we were called to be. Our vocation continues, even though some of us may choose to stop working. In fact, for some of us, especially those who have found their work situations difficult, who weren't able to use all or even some of their gifts in their careers, retirement may be the time in life to live out vocation fully. It may be the opportunity we've been waiting for our entire lives.

MY FATHER, I would say, is a good example of someone who waited a long time to pursue his vocation. He was born with an artistic gift, and from an early age it was clear that he could draw. While other children were drawing stick figures, he was sketching people. It must have been stunning for his parents and teachers to witness this. I've seen a few of his drawings from childhood, and I'm in awe of his raw talent.

My father is quick to point out that not all of his drawing ability was simply there at birth. He worked at his gift and developed it over the years. He even went to school to refine it.

Like other people his age (what Tom Brokaw has called "the greatest generation"), my father put duty to country and family ahead of himself. He answered the call of his country and served in the Navy during World War II. After that, he went into business to make a life — quite a comfortable one too, as I remember it — for his family. For most of his adult life, art was on hold. He did a little (a surprising amount, really, for someone with other primary demands on his time), but nothing close to his capacity.

One day — and it came as quite a shock to the family — he walked away from the business to which he had devoted forty years of his life and which he owned by that point. He walked away in order to fully embrace his calling, what he considered to be his *true* vocation.

For the last twenty years he's been painting watercolors (primarily) with the same energy and passion that he used to devote to his advertising business. But now, you see, it's different. Now it seems clear to everyone who knows him that he's finally pursuing his calling in life. He is using his gift to uncover and then point to the beauty of our world, often in stunning Lake Michigan settings, but sometimes in totally unexpected places as well. It's a service to God, and it's also a service to anyone who looks for beauty in creation.

THERE'S A LESSON to be learned from individuals like my father. There may come a point when change is finally possible. As always, there are many factors to consider before making a move, but we need to be ready for the opportunity when it comes along.

In an earlier chapter I argued that midlife was a time when options tended to narrow and that the vocational work of midlife was to come to terms with those losses, to accept them (gracefully, if possible), and to move on. I still think that's true. What I'm suggesting here is different. Though our options almost always narrow as we grow older, I believe that there's often time later in our lives to do what God has called us and gifted us to do. In my experience, this is far from being one last, desperate attempt at something. Many people I know have reported feeling an enormous sense of freedom at this point in their lives, the freedom to respond fully and at long last.

Blessing and Wisdom

Not all of us have a career in art to look forward to when we retire. But there is a vocation just about all of us could embrace as we get older.

We may think of ourselves as retired at a certain point, especially when we leave our jobs behind, but there is an important calling that transcends retirement.

I stumbled on this particular calling one day when I was reading the book of Proverbs in preparation for a class I was teaching. Proverbs contains a fair amount of useful instruction — for those who have the courage to read it. What I mean is that some parts of the book are surprisingly and painfully direct. One bit of direct wisdom is about older adults. According to Proverbs, they are blessed with two important characteristics: they are the people in our lives who give wisdom and blessing.

Proverbs 20:29 puts it somewhat cryptically: "The glory of youths is their strength, but the beauty of the aged is their gray hair." I think the point is that life experience is or at least can be quite powerful. If youth have strength on their side, the more mature among us have the wisdom that comes with long life.

Older adulthood may be the time in life when losses pile up, but what we don't lose as we get older is the gift of being able to impart blessing and wisdom.

Now, the problem is — and I'm beginning to sense this rather acutely in my own life, just as I'm reaching the point when I might have some wisdom to offer — that fewer and fewer people want to hear it. Here I'm thinking particularly of conversations with my kids. I've learned the hard way never to start a sentence with "When I was your age . . ." If you do, you'll learn, as I did, that your pearl of wisdom will, as the Bible puts it, disappear before swine. What you did at their age is of no consequence to them whatsoever.

I'm finding this to be true professionally as well. After twenty-five years of ministry, you might think that I have a certain amount of pastoral wisdom to pass on. There isn't much I haven't seen or experienced along the way. Unfortunately — and I'm guessing this is true in other fields or professions as well — ministry has changed so much over the years that my pearls of wisdom don't always count for very much.

After all, what was true in ministry when I started isn't always true today. Seminary students can see that the church has changed significantly. Most of the time, to their credit, they're ready to try new ideas and fresh approaches. Besides, they sometimes argue, people of my generation clearly got it wrong as often as we got it right. So sometimes what I've learned along the way isn't always helpful to people who are just starting out — or it isn't always received eagerly.

So here's what I want you to see. Our real authority as we grow older, our most important gift to the people who are coming along behind us, our real strength, is our power to bless. By blessing I mean encouragement, affirmation, support, and so on. The people who are younger than we are *hunger* for our blessing, even when they don't appear to want our wisdom, and blessing is what we need to give them.

They can survive without it, of course, but they will thrive with it. For some it can make all the difference.

I HAVE a retired pastor friend. I get to see him nearly every summer when my family is on vacation. Typically we find an hour or so just to talk and catch up. He seeks me out, in fact, soon after my family moves into the cottage we rent most summers.

> "The blessings of your father are stronger than the blessings of the eternal mountains, the bounties of the everlasting hills; may they be on the head of Joseph, on the brow of him who was set apart from his brothers."
>
> Genesis 49:26

But every year the conversation moves in basically the same distressing direction. He tells me what a sorry state the church is in. Not my church, of course — he's usually careful about that — but the church in general. He knows this, he says, because he still gets around. He still does a little preaching now and then when active pastors, like me, are on vacation. As far as he's concerned, the church has been on a downward slide toward mediocrity ever since he retired.

To be honest, I don't look forward to these conversations. I don't find them very uplifting, particularly when I'm on vacation and hoping to leave a few of the annoyances of parish ministry behind.

One summer, after I published my first book, I brought a copy with me to the lake and proudly gave it to him when we got together. After I handed it to him, I stood there waiting for his congratulations. All he said — and all he has ever said to me about that book — was, "Well, I'm glad you got *that* out of your system!"

If I could screw up the courage, I would tell him that his complaints about the church just plain get me down. If only he could find a way to use his considerable experience and wisdom to bless me, to bless *something* about the work I do, if he could find a way to bless the other young (or middle-aged) pastors he talks to, I'm guessing we would all gladly listen to him.

It seems clear to me that he needs me and the validation I provide him. In a way, I honor him by listening to him each summer. What he doesn't seem to understand is that I also need him. I would delight in his blessing. And if I felt his blessing, I think I would seek out his wisdom.

IF YOU'RE an older adult and you have all kinds of life experience, if you've seen and done a great deal with your life, you have a vocation even in retirement, a vocation I challenge you to take seriously, perhaps more seriously than you have until this point. One of the ways you could live out your vocation would be to offer wisdom and blessing to people who are younger than you are — your children and grandchildren, of course, but others too, anyone you meet in the course of your life.

But here's my suggestion: Start with blessing. Find *someone* to bless. In other words, find someone who's hungry for your encouragement, affirmation, and support. All of us are, so this part shouldn't be difficult. When you give this person the affirmation he needs, I'm guessing that you'll be amazed at the way he begins to seek out your wisdom.

Funny how it works that way.

I CAN'T resist adding this one last story. Since I described the retired pastor who doesn't get it right, I think I should describe someone who does. Get it right, that is.

One Sunday, as I was greeting at the door of my church, a white-haired man with a kindly smile thanked me for my sermon. "That was the best sermon I've ever heard on that text," he told me. When I thanked him and asked him who he was, he told me that he was a retired pastor who had just moved to a retirement facility within a few miles of my church.

Over the next few years, I came to know him much better. Every time he left church through the door where I was greeting, he had a word of encouragement for me. I could count on him. Even when I knew that my sermon hadn't been one of my best, or hadn't been delivered to the best of my ability, he found something to say that was affirming and supportive. Many Sundays I needed to hear what he had to say.

During one of our conversations, I asked him about his move to the retirement facility. He said he was somewhat sad about it and recognized that it was probably the last move of his life, but then he brightened and said, "This is my new parish. This is the place where God has called me to serve."

For the rest of his life, my friend and colleague fulfilled his vocation as a pastor — to me, to members of my church, and to every person he encountered. At his memorial service, I listened as people who knew him told story after story about a kind, gentle, loving man who never really retired. His vocation transcended his retirement. And what's more, he understood his calling that way. He was called to serve, and he never stopped.

WHAT ABOUT YOU? Where will you find meaning and purpose in retirement? What will your vocation be when you take your well-deserved break from a lifetime of work?

QUESTIONS FOR REFLECTION AND DISCUSSION

1. Describe in a single sentence what you believe your calling in life really is. How much of your calling are you able to pursue right now in your job or career? What gifts are you able to use in your work? What are the gifts that are currently going unused?

2. If you're an older adult, is there a call you haven't pursued before that you could begin to consider now? What is it that you have always felt

called to do with your life and your gifts? What would it take to make the change and begin to pursue this other path?

3. Who are the people in your life who need and want your blessing? Are there people in your life who seem to resist the wisdom you try to pass along to them? Could you imagine yourself blessing them? What would you say? What do you suppose the response would be?

CHAPTER 8

What Can I Learn from Others? Listening to Stories

Very early in my ministry I became aware that the pastoral role invited and assumed intimacy. At the beginning I don't know that I was prepared for it. I don't see how anyone could be. But I quickly learned that people see a pastor as someone who will listen, who is *expected* to listen. Without much encouragement people will open their hearts and tell their stories to a pastor.

Some of the stories I have heard are profoundly and disturbingly sad. After all, it's usually people in distress who need to talk to a pastor. But not all of the stories I hear are sad. Some are inspiring, deeply so, and when I hear one of those, I'm grateful for the kind of work that allows me simply to listen.

But there are still other stories that can't be labeled simply as either sad or inspiring. In the course of my work I've heard stories that are both of those things — and much more. When I hear one of those — and I don't hear them often, but when I do — I find something about my own life changed. My own sense of vocation is altered and enriched.

What follows are three stories that have changed my life in some fundamental way, stories that have challenged me to live differently as a result of hearing them. They are multifaceted stories about call or vocation, stories about people whose life decisions have certainly brought, in the words of Reformed scholar Neal Plantinga, "good growth for the kingdom."

John O'Melia

I first met John O'Melia when I was serving a church in New Jersey. He and a group of people from Illinois had traveled to hear me preach and to take me out to lunch afterward for a conversation about coming to their church in Wheaton, Illinois (an invitation I was later to accept). John was the oldest member of the group — and clearly a person who was held in high regard by the rest of the group. I sensed that there was something special about John the first time I met him, but it wasn't until later that I first heard, *really* heard, the story of his life.

A few years after John and I met, my wife, Susan, and I led a study tour to Israel, and John and his wife, Marty, were a part of our group. One day, while touring in Jerusalem, our group stopped at the Yad Vashem museum, which is an important Holocaust memorial and exhibit.

Soon after we entered the building, I noticed that John wasn't feeling well, and I decided to follow him out to our air-conditioned tour bus and sit with him there. He was pale and sweaty, but he insisted that he was going to be okay. And it was then that he began to tell me his story, a story that he hadn't told many other people up to that point in his life.

John had finished a couple of years at a Presbyterian college in western Pennsylvania when he and most of his male classmates decided that it was time to enlist in the army. World War II was already underway, and John had a pretty good idea where he would be going and what he would be asked to do when he got there.

As a soldier in General Patton's now-famous Third Army, John was part of the Allied advance across Europe. He saw a considerable amount of fighting along the way, as the retreating German forces put up an often-deadly resistance. At one point, he told me, he took a camera from a dead German soldier, an object that soon became more than a memento: he used it to document the last, disturbing days of the war.

Before a final, deadly push into Germany, an army chaplain led John and a group of soldiers in a battlefield communion service that turned out to be particularly memorable. The chaplain spoke that day about the hope of a resurrection to eternal life, and John, now in his eighties, remembers much of what the chaplain said. The men listened intently, as I imagine I would have in a similar setting.

Within a few days, the forces John was with entered the Nazi death camp known as Dachau. He was one of the first to see the hundreds of corpses stacked like firewood waiting for the ovens. John told me of freeing some children who were held in what looked like chicken coops. They were too weak and frightened to break down the flimsy enclosure on their own.

THE PICTURES John showed me later, back in the States, confirmed what I had previously read about the Nazi death camps. It's hard for me to imagine being nineteen or twenty years old and having to witness what John had to see that day.

At some point toward the end of that first day in the camp, filled as it was with both horror and nausea, John went off by himself for some personal reflection. He remembers kneeling and saying to God that he wanted to devote his life to making sure something like this never happened again. For John the best way — maybe the only way — to deal with what he had seen was to offer his life in service to God and neighbor.

After the war John made good on his promise. He finished his college degree and took a job with the YMCA, where he spent the rest of his working life. He held a variety of positions with the Y, from being part of an inner-city branch in Cleveland to serving on the international board, but his vocation remained the same. He worked tirelessly throughout his life for racial reconciliation and understanding.

In the 1950s John organized one of the country's first fully integrated summer camping programs, which at the time required great courage and vision. As his career unfolded, John traveled the world on behalf of the Y, and on the trips we took together, long after his retirement, I witnessed the warm embraces he received from old friends and acquaintances. On a single day I observed John enthusiastically welcomed first at the Y in East Jerusalem and then later at the Y on the Israeli side.

A few years ago John was elected to the YMCA Hall of Fame, an honor he didn't have in mind when he first decided what his calling was, but something he richly deserved. In retirement John continues to work at his vocation. At the annual worship services we held in Wheaton on Martin Luther King Jr. Day, his was always one of the faces I saw.

> Even as every Christian is called to love God and neighbor, so each Christian is called to offer her or his life to serve God's shalom. In all their callings — home and extended family, friendships, paid work, cultural activity, and political life — Christians must strive to establish justice, contribute to the common good, and promote enjoyment in creation under God's reign.
>
> Douglas J. Schuurman, *Vocation: Discerning Our Callings in Life*

As John sees it, it's part of his vocation to attend, so he plans to go to those services for as long as he's able.

Henrieta Ribiero

Henrieta Ribiero, also a member of my church in Wheaton, Illinois, grew up in what was then Czechoslovakia and came to the United States to study at Wheaton College. Today she's married and has a practice in clinical psychology. When she arrived in the States her last name was Krupova, a family name that deserves to be better known than it is.

Henrieta's grandparents were Protestants, part of a Christian tradition in eastern Europe that dates back to the Reformation and before. When the Communists came to power shortly after World War II, Henrieta's grandfather struggled with his call to be a good citizen. He took very seriously the Apostle Paul's words in Romans 13 ("Let every person be subject to the governing authorities, for there is no authority except from God, and those authorities that exist have been instituted by God").

According to the law at that time, there was, nominally at least, freedom of religion, so Henrieta's grandfather openly distributed Bibles and other Christian literature. Bible smugglers from the West knew Henrieta's grandfather, and they would bring their materials to his home. He did the rest, and his work eventually — inevitably — came to the attention of the secret police.

One day, on his way home from work, Henrieta's grandfather was arrested and imprisoned — not for his church work, which was technically legal, but for embezzling money from his employer, a trumped-up charge. In prison he was sent to work in a uranium mine, which was essentially a death sentence. After three years he became very ill and was sent home to die. Once home, however, he continued to pursue his calling — which was witnessing to his faith through the distribution of Christian literature.

Before his death, Henrieta says, he was able to see the collapse of the Communist government, a day he thought would never come. It was one of the happiest days of his life.

THERE'S MORE to the story of Henrieta's family. Her father was an extraordinarily gifted student, and he dreamed of one day becoming a physicist. But only party members were permitted to attend university, and so for a long time this educational door was closed to him.

Finally, in 1968, during the so-called Prague spring, an opportunity presented itself, and Henrieta's father traveled to England. There he attended Oxford University, and he earned his Ph.D. in physics.

When he returned to Czechoslovakia, he accepted a teaching position, and with his family he became active in church life. Church building was once again being permitted, but only under the strictest — some might say ridiculous — rules. Construction, for example, could take place only at night. There could be no construction equipment on the building site. And all building had to be below ground. In other words, it would be illegal for a church structure to be taller than any surrounding buildings.

Not to be deterred, Henrieta's family and other church members actually built a church underground. They basically dug the hole for the church structure with their hands. They worked at night, often through the night, to observe the government's rules. When they were finished, they had met the all-but-impossible requirements for construction. The last row of the balcony, as Henrieta describes it, was at street level.

Today, of course, the Communist government is gone, but the underground church remains. And according to Henrieta, who visits the church whenever she visits her family, it is a thriving congregation. The faithful witness of the church members during years of harassment and persecution caught the attention of numerous people.

> A Christian looks at even the smaller decisions . . . with faith and good humor, aware that in the plan of God, the mustard seed of one of our decisions may combine with the mustard seed of others' decisions to bring good growth for the kingdom.
>
> Cornelius Plantinga Jr.,
> *Engaging God's World*

During all those years, Henrieta's family thought of their church membership as a calling. And it was a calling they took seriously in the face of intimidation, sacrifice, and imprisonment. Occasionally, when I feel sorry for myself because my work isn't going quite as well as I'd like, I think of the testimony of Henrieta's family. And then my own difficulties pale into insignificance.

Elias Chacour

Before my first trip to Israel, I asked the thirty or so people who were going to make the trip with me to read a book by a Palestinian Christian and priest named Elias Chacour. Most of them had never heard of him, and to tell the truth, I didn't know much about him, either. But I thought we should learn as much as we could about the situation in that troubled land — from as many different perspectives as possible.

My plan was to lead the group off the usual tourist path to a school that Father Chacour had founded in a tiny, dusty village in the Galilee region of Israel known as Ibillin. I wanted the group to see more than ancient Roman ruins; I wanted them to engage the politics of the region. As it turned out, visitors to Israel can't help but engage those politics. But I didn't know that at the time.

By going to Father Chacour's school and perhaps by meeting some of his students, I hoped our group would learn something of the plight of Christians in that part of the world. The Western media give a great deal of attention to Jewish and Muslim perspectives, but relatively little is known about Christian groups in that part of the world, many of whom have lived there for centuries.

What I wasn't quite prepared for was the time we were able to spend with Father Chacour himself. After our tour bus drove up a steep hill to the school, it was Father Chacour himself who met us and directed us to a classroom, where he spoke to us for more than an hour. The story of his life engages me as powerfully today as it did the first time I heard it.

Blood Brothers is the title of Father Chacour's first book, and it's a moving autobiographical account of his life in a country that most

American Christians know as the Holy Land. In the book Father Chacour describes the arrival in 1948 of Israeli forces in Biram, a tiny Galilean village that is Father Chacour's ancestral home. The Israelis immediately rounded up his father and older brothers, to take them to a refugee camp. As he was being taken away, Father Chacour's father told young Elias not to turn to violence, but to remember the example of Jesus, which turned out to be a lesson in forgiveness and compassion that Father Chacour has never forgotten.

The village of Biram, including the grove of olive trees tended by the Chacour family for generations, was destroyed. For a time young Elias lived with his mother in a neighboring village — until a bishop in the Melkite tradition encouraged the boy, who showed considerable promise as a student, to study abroad.

After receiving his theological degrees in Paris and turning down a number of opportunities to teach at European universities, he returned to Galilee and was ordained a priest. His first assignment — not a promising start for someone so bright and well-educated — was to a small village called Ibillin. The bishop told Father Chacour that the assignment would be brief — for the summer, maybe, but no longer.

For most of that summer Father Chacour slept in his car. But he decided he could tolerate anything if it was only for a few months. As things turned out, the months became years. Father Chacour has never left Ibillin.

TODAY, IN ADDITION to the small parish church, there is now a large and growing school in Ibillin founded by Father Chacour. It's called the Mar Elias Educational Institutions. Christian, Jewish, Muslim, and Druze children — kindergarten through high school — study together and learn the way of peace by attending classes together and hearing the story of Jesus' life. A university, also a dream of Father Chacour and currently under construction nearby, will be the only Arab university in northern Israel.

When the idea of starting the school first came to Father Chacour, the Israeli government refused to issue a building permit. He had the vision, the money, the students, even the faculty — what he couldn't get was the permit. At the risk of having the government bulldoze the school after it had been constructed — something officials threatened to do — Father Chacour decided to go ahead and build anyway.

As he puts it, with a smile, "*We* needed the school. It was the government that needed the permit."

Still, Father Chacour remained fearful of the Israeli government's intention toward his work. Finally he traveled to the United States and went to the Washington D.C. home of then-Secretary of State James Baker. He pleaded with Baker's wife, Susan, to ask her husband to intervene with the Israeli government on behalf of the school. It was a bold move, but it worked. James Baker got the school its building permit. In fact, he was so impressed by the determination of this Palestinian priest that he and Susan were present for the dedication of the building.

Father Chacour, always remembering the words of his father, has dedicated his life to peace in a land torn by war. Along the way, he has received many prizes and honors, including three nominations for the Nobel Peace Prize. He has also been named Archbishop of Israel.

Three Stories, Three Vocations

John O'Melia, Henrieta Ribiero, Elias Chacour — when I hear and think about their stories and others like them, I find myself understanding more clearly and deeply what my faith tells me about vocation, what it tells me about *my* vocation. I know that vocation is more than a job and larger than a career. What's often difficult for me to understand is exactly how much larger. All of life — everything we do with our lives — can be considered a response to God's call. But that's often a difficult concept to grasp without a story to bring it to life.

For John O'Melia, the call has been to build bridges of understanding between different and sometimes hostile racial groups. For Henrieta Ribiero and her family, the call has been to remain faithful and to persevere in the face of government persecution. For Elias Chacour, the call is to claim the example of Jesus and the way of peace, when all around him is the temptation to abandon hope and turn to violence. Obviously, these are calls that go far beyond job or career. And one characteristic they all share is a life-changing event or experience that calls for a response, a *vocational* response.

Few of us have experienced war or oppression, but all — or most — of us have been through difficult times. Pushed by circumstances, and sometimes by larger historical events, we have had to respond. And what I've learned from the stories of my friends is that that these experiences can sometimes be occasions for being called — not to job or career, but to something more.

In the last chapter I want to describe what this "something more" might be. I've referred several times to being a part of something larger than ourselves, and now it's time to say exactly what I mean.

QUESTIONS FOR REFLECTION AND DISCUSSION

1. What is the story of *your* life? What has shaped and defined you? Have you ever taken the time to reflect on some of the key events of your life and how you responded to them? If you viewed them as providing you with a call, how has your life been shaped or changed?

2. In *Engaging God's World,* Neal Plantinga writes that even our smaller decisions can be occasions for bringing "good growth for the kingdom." How have some of the smaller decisions of your life fit into the larger picture of God's work?

3. Church membership, citizenship, even marriage and family — among other things — play a role in the way we live out our vocations. What are the ways — beyond job and career — you live out your vocation?

CHAPTER 9

How Can I Be a Co-Creator with God?

A few years ago my wife, Susan, and I took our older daughter to college. I had known that she was leaving home for quite a while, but nothing could have prepared me for the pain and grief of that separation. I had heard other parents talk about it, but until it happened to me I had no idea how awful it would be.

The year leading up to her departure was actually quite exciting. As a family we visited several colleges and enjoyed some extended family time together, something that becomes all too rare as kids get older. I remember our trip to the college she eventually chose. Our visit was relatively late in the process; applications had to be mailed in just a few weeks. Still, the visit was a wonderful one. She and I walked across the campus together, and I knew — from her smile, from the sound of her voice, from the way she walked — that we had found the right college for her. I was thrilled — for her, for myself, for everything. I was deliriously happy.

I was also in deep denial.

The Labor Day weekend when we dropped her off at her dormitory, I kept fighting back the tears. At one point during the unloading process, the men's cross-country team ran by, without shirts, and I noticed that my daughter was tracking them all the way across the campus. At that point I knew — as if I needed any further reminders — that my role in her life was different. She loved me, but she was moving out and moving on. Things had changed.

I tried not to cry until Susan and I were in the car and off campus. On the way home we drove in silence for several hours. Every few miles, as I thought of my daughter and the times we had enjoyed together, tears welled up, and I sobbed.

Once my wife and I arrived home, we closed the door of our daughter's bedroom and realized that we couldn't look inside for several days. The first baby we had brought home from the hospital was now gone. Our little family was never going to be the same. I couldn't imagine the future without her.

A Picture of the Future

One temptation in a time of grief is to romanticize the past. The truth is, living with a teenager is no picnic. Family dinner times weren't happening all that often anymore, and my daughter wasn't always forthcoming about how she was doing or how she was feeling. But still. I was painfully aware that *something* important was coming to an end, and my grief prevented me from seeing anything but my own loss.

I had no mental picture of what the future might look like, and this compounded the feeling of loss. A few difficult months later, however, a new picture began to come into focus. I started to see what the future was going to be like. Kids do come home again. It's not like before, but they do come back. They breeze into town, sleep for long stretches at a time, see friends, do large quantities of laundry, and are often surprisingly kind and grateful to their parents.

Life does go on. I couldn't see it at the time of separation, but I can see it now. Some parents have told me that relationships in these situations improve and deepen. Conversations with their children become rich and textured. Separation creates an intensity that was unknown in the years leading up to college.

What I want to suggest in this chapter is that all of us — not just parents of college students, but all of us — need a picture of the future in order to keep going, in order to live with hope and expectation. No matter how clear we may be about our vocations, no matter how certain we may be about our particular gifts, there will be days when the work is hard, progress is slow, and hope is in short supply. And on those days especially, we need to remember the big picture, how our efforts combine with the efforts of so many others to accomplish God's plan.

I believe that people of faith have been given such a picture of the future.

Anyone who has attended worship services during Advent and has listened to the great texts of Isaiah's prophecy has been given a wonderful picture of the future:

> The wolf shall live with the lamb,
>> the leopard shall lie down with the kid,
> the calf and the lion and the fatling together,
>> and a little child shall lead them.
>
> Isaiah 11:6

> Then the eyes of the blind shall be opened,
>> and the ears of the deaf unstopped;
> then the lame shall leap like a deer,
>> and the tongue of the speechless sing for joy.
> For waters shall break forth in the wilderness,
>> and streams in the desert;
> the burning sand shall become a pool,
>> and the thirsty ground springs of water. . . .
>
> Isaiah 35:5-7a

Nicholas Wolterstorff, a well-known philosopher who for the past number of years was at Yale University, has taught and written extensively about shalom. His words have inspired a new generation of scholars — and preachers — to teach and write about shalom as well.

In this concluding chapter I want to lift up shalom as the compelling picture of our future, the future God has in mind for us. It's a picture that keeps us going and ultimately one that gives meaning and purpose to our lives, just as it did for the people of Israel long ago.

As Wolterstorff and now others have described it, the word "shalom" is a more complete word than, say, "peace," though that of course is its most frequent and popular translation. Shalom might best be defined as an ideal, described in poetic terms by Old Testament prophets. In shalom, peace and justice come together. But more than that, peace combines with delight and enjoyment in right relationships — with God, with self, with fellow humans, and with nature.

In shalom, there is peace, but not peace without justice. There is justice, but not justice without enjoyment. In shalom, as Isaiah and others imagined it, the whole creation will come together in such a way that we will delight in each other, in God, and in nature itself.

I like Wolterstorff's way of describing it in his book *Until Justice and Peace Embrace:*

> In shalom there are no blind, all see; in shalom there are no lame, all walk; there are no deaf, all hear; there are no dead, all live. And, there are no poor; all have plenty. To be impoverished is to fall short of shalom. That is what is wrong with poverty. God is committed to shalom. Jesus came to bring shalom. In shalom there is no poverty. . . . As the prince of shalom, Jesus could not avoid taking the side of the poor against the rich.

In theological terms, what's happening is that God is in the process of restoring creation to the way it was intended to be. God created things good, very good, but things have gone terribly wrong —

so wrong, in fact, that at times it's difficult, if not impossible, to see any sign of God's hand in creation. But God loves his creation so much that things will not continue as they are. People of faith believe — this is our hope — that God is at work right now, reclaiming what is lost.

And we, God's people, are called to be co-creators in the effort. Expressed in the broadest possible terms, that's our vocation.

Our lives, our work, our time here on earth have all been co-opted by God for no less a purpose than to assist God with the ongoing work of creation. We are engaged in an enterprise that God is determined to complete in and through us.

> Shalom is the human being dwelling at peace in all his or her relationships: with God, with self, with fellows, with nature. . . . But the peace which is shalom is not entirely the absence of hostility, not merely being in right relationship. Shalom at its highest is enjoyment in one's relationships. . . . To dwell in shalom is to enjoy living before God, to enjoy living in one's physical surroundings, to enjoy living with one's fellows, to enjoy life with oneself.
>
> Nicholas Wolterstorff,
> *Until Justice and Peace Embrace*

Really, it's an astonishing thought, isn't it? It takes my breath away when I think about it. This picture gives me hope and new energy in moments when my spirit is sagging. It's a vision that compels me to offer my best because it's worthy of my best. After all, so much is at stake.

Good Growth for the Kingdom

In the past it was common for Christian writers and theologians to place vocation within the larger category of creation and to speak of vocation solely in terms of God's plan or design for our lives.

More recent scholars have argued that vocation really belongs within the larger category of eschatology, which refers to Christian teachings about the future. In other words, if God is in the process, even now, of reclaiming creation and restoring it to the way it was intended to be, then our calling to participate with God in that project has eschatological significance. The future in some ways depends on us and God's work through us. What we do with our lives matters and has meaning because of our role in God's ongoing work.

I like this way of thinking because it emphasizes the importance of our work — not our work for its own sake, but for the difference it can make. Even the small, seemingly insignificant decisions we make matter. They have a cumulative effect. We may not be able to do everything, and our contributions may not be huge. But, taken together, they add up.

This way of thinking affects how I feel about the work I do. The hospital visit I make late on a Friday afternoon, the encouraging word I offer to a member of my staff who is struggling, the prayer I offer before yet another committee meeting — these actions, taken together, amount to something. Over the long haul, my life is making a difference. I may not

> For surely I know the plans I have for you, says the LORD, plans for your welfare and not for harm, to give you a future with hope.
>
> Jeremiah 29:11, NRSV

even be able to see it — and most days I confess that I can't — but I work with the hope and reassurance that I am participating in an enterprise of staggering importance.

IN 2004 I SAID good-bye to my congregation in Wheaton, Illinois, which I had served for thirteen years. The farewell was tearful and full of emotion, almost more than I could handle. We enjoyed a rich season of ministry together.

What made a powerful impression on me, as I listened to individual members say good-bye, was their memories of my work. They thanked me for my preaching, of course, and my teaching, and sometimes my visits to the hospital. But what they remembered and cherished most were the little things: small exchanges at the door of the sanctuary, tiny bits of conversation between services, a supportive hug in the hallway.

One person never forgot that I remembered his name after his first visit to the church. A young person recalled how I had personally challenged him to read a favorite book of mine, and how he had challenged me in return to read a favorite book of his. Still another person remembered the time we sat on the curb together and watched Wheaton's Fourth of July parade.

To be perfectly honest, I had forgotten most of these interactions. At the time, apparently, they didn't seem all that important — not compared to what I considered to be my more important work of preaching, teaching, writing, and pastoral care. This occasion reminded me that even our briefest interactions with each other have enormous potential for good, for giving life, for creating the sort of world that God intended.

And no one needs ordination to offer kindness and love. We all share in this vocation.

IN THE PREVIOUS chapter I quoted from Neal Plantinga's fine book entitled *Engaging God's World,* where he speaks of making choices, vocational choices, that will "bring good growth for the kingdom." I like that phrase for many reasons, but primarily because it's a reminder that our vocational choices are not, finally, about us.

The "do what you love and the money will follow" approach to vocational decision-making assumes that life is, finally, about us and our happiness. Faith, *Christian* faith, always calls us beyond ourselves. It reminds us that our lives are all about God and God's purposes, that we are giving ourselves over to God's life.

There are days when we need to remind ourselves that we are about God's work in the world and that our work really does matter in the overall scheme of things.

ONE MORNING on my way to work, I turned on the radio and listened to an interview with a retired air force general, the last prisoner of war from the Vietnam era to retire from active duty in the military — after forty years of service. According to the reporter, the general had reached the mandatory retirement age of sixty-two and was reluctantly stepping aside after a distinguished career.

What struck me most about the interview was the general's ability to see his work as part of something larger than himself. He explained that during his six years in prison after being shot down over North Vietnam, he had an unwavering belief in the importance of his mission. Solitary confinement, beatings, and torture only served to strengthen his resolve.

There were days — not many, but a few — when he would feel sorry for himself. But then he would remember, he said, who he was and what he had signed up to do. In all the years since his release he has counted himself privileged to be part of a fine institution like the air force. His pride in a mission larger than himself was all but palpable. As he brought his career to an end, he spoke with admiration for the people around him and for the institution they serve.

A voice cries out:
"In the wilderness prepare the way of the LORD,
make straight in the desert a highway for our God.
Every valley shall be lifted up,
and every mountain and hill be made low;
the uneven ground shall become level,
and the rough places a plain."

Isaiah 40:3-4, NRSV

I don't remember the general's name anymore, but I won't forget his example. I would love to have that same clear sense of commitment and purpose about what I do, wouldn't you?

Let me ask you: Whose uniform do you wear? To whom do you swear your ultimate allegiance? For what purpose are you willing to give your life?

IN THESE chapters I've described vocation in some very personal terms, though the truth is, it's hardly a personal endeavor. Certainly there are levels at which vocation is personal. The process of discernment, for example, of listening for God's call in our lives, is sometimes highly personal.

Even so, vocation is always going to be about something that is bigger than ourselves; the focus is never self-centered. For people of faith, vocation is always going to be directed outward (to God and neighbor), not inward.

"A voice cries out: 'In the wilderness prepare the way of the LORD, make straight in the desert a highway for our God.'" I don't know what you hear when these words from Isaiah are read, but I hear words that are addressed directly to me. My life has been given to me to prepare the way of the Lord, to make a highway in the desert.

What about you? What have you been called to do with *your* life?

QUESTIONS FOR REFLECTION AND DISCUSSION

1. Sometimes a mental picture of the way things ought to be (or will one day be) helps us to face the future. Can you think of places in your life where the future has not yet arrived and where a picture of the future is helping you to cope?

2. Isaiah doesn't provide many specifics. His words are deliberately suggestive. Have you ever tried to imagine what shalom will be like? This is important to think about, because your picture of shalom will determine your vocational thinking. What will the future look like? What sort of world is God using you to usher in?

3. Our small choices and decisions have a cumulative effect for the kingdom of God. Look back over the last week and think of some choices, large and small, that you made and ask yourself how they contributed to the work of God. How could you begin to choose differently, to live more effectively?

Bibliography

Adrienne, Carol. *The Purpose of Your Experiential Guide: The Proven Program to Help You Find Your Reason for Being.* New York: William Morrow, 1999.

Badcock, Gary D. *A Theology of Christian Vocation.* Grand Rapids: Wm. B. Eerdmans, 1998.

Bolles, Richard Nelson. *What Color Is Your Parachute? A Practical Manual for Job-Hunters and Career-Changers.* Berkeley, Calif.: Ten Speed Press, 2004.

Buechner, Frederick. *Wishful Thinking: A Seeker's ABC.* New York: Harper & Row, 1973.

Calhoun, Robert Lowry. *God and the Day's Work: Christian Vocation in an Unchristian World.* New York: Association Press, 1957.

Campolo, Anthony. *You Can Make a Difference.* Waco, Tex.: Word Press, 1984.

Coles, Robert. *The Call of Service: A Witness to Idealism.* Boston: Houghton Mifflin, 1993.

Finney, Martha. *Find Your Calling, Love Your Life.* New York: Simon & Schuster, 1998.

Fowler, James W. *Becoming Adult, Becoming Christian: Adult Development and Christian Faith.* San Francisco: Jossey-Bass, 2000.

Guinness, Os. *The Call: Finding and Fulfilling the Central Purpose of Your Life.* Nashville: Word Press, 1998.

Hardy, Lee J. *The Fabric of This World: Inquiries into Calling, Career Choice, and the Design of Human Work.* Grand Rapids: Wm. B. Eerdmans, 1990.

Holderness, Ginny Ward. *Career and Calling: A Guide for Counselors, Youth, and Young Adults.* Louisville: Geneva Press, 2001.

Hybels, Bill, and Rob Wilkins. *Descending into Greatness.* Grand Rapids: Zondervan Publishing House, 1993.

Krueger, David A. *Keeping Faith at Work: The Christian in the Workplace.* Nashville: Abingdon Press, 1994.

Leider, Richard J. *The Power of Purpose: Creating Meaning in Your Life and Work.* San Francisco: Berrett-Koehler Publishers, 1997.

Leider, Richard J., and David A. Shapiro. *Whistle While You Work: Heeding Your Life's Calling.* San Francisco: Berrett-Koehler Publishers, 2001.

Lewis, Roy. *Choosing Your Career, Finding Your Vocation: A Step-by-Step Guide for Adults and Counselors.* New York: Paulist Press, 1989.

Mahen, Brian. *Forgetting Ourselves on Purpose.* San Francisco: Jossey-Bass, 2002.

Novak, Michael. *Business as a Calling: Work and the Examined Life.* New York: Simon & Schuster, 1996.

Palmer, Parker J. *The Active Life: Wisdom for Work, Creativity, and Caring.* New York: Harper & Row, 1990.

————. *Let Your Life Speak: Listening for the Voice of Vocation.* San Francisco: Jossey-Bass, 2000.

Plantinga, Cornelius Jr. *Engaging God's World: A Christian Vision of Faith, Learning, and Living.* Grand Rapids: Wm. B. Eerdmans, 2003.

Schultze, Quentin. *Here I Am: Now What on Earth Should I Be Doing?* Grand Rapids: Baker Book House, 2005.

Schuurman, Douglas J. *Vocation: Discerning Our Callings in Life.* Grand Rapids: Wm. B. Eerdmans, 2004.

Smith, Gordon T. *Courage and Calling: Embracing Your God-Given Potential.* Downers Grove, Ill.: InterVarsity Press, 1999.

Stevens, R. Paul. *The Other Six Days: Vocation, Work, and Ministry in Biblical Perspective.* Grand Rapids: Wm. B. Eerdmans, 1999.

Trueblood, Elton. *Your Other Vocation.* New York: Harper, 1952.

Veith, Gene Edward Jr. *God at Work: The Spirituality of Ordinary Life.* Wheaton, Ill.: Crossway Books, 2002.

Weiler, Nicholas W., and Stephen C. Schoonover. *Your Soul at Work: Five Steps to a More Fulfilling Career and Life.* Mahwah, N.J.: Hidden Spring, 2000.

Wingren, Gustaf. *The Christian's Calling.* Edinburgh: Oliver & Boyd, 1958.

Wolterstorff, Nicholas. *Until Justice and Peace Embrace.* Grand Rapids: Wm. B. Eerdmans, 1983.

Zehring, John William. *Making Your Life Count: Finding Fulfillment Beyond Your Job.* Valley Forge, Pa.: Judson Press, 1980.